# SIMPLY HEALTHY.

*Copyright © 2013*

**The Delgado Protocol**
Books may be purchased for educational use.
For information to order single copies or for
multiple copy discounts write to:

**The Delgado Protocol**
711 W. 17th St. #H6
Costa Mesa 92627

First Edition

ISBN 978-1-61920-011-1

Photography and Graphic Design by **LuvMouse.com** *(They also do videos)*
Recipes Prepared by: **Chef Ramon McCormick**

**Manufactured in the United States of America**

# FOREWARD...

Good health is our birthright. We should live our years actively, in lean, light bodies, with abundant energy, flexibility and muscular strength throughout our lifespan. Along with sensible exercise and emotional happiness, proper diet is essential in creating a state of vibrant health. Fortunately, much progress has been made towards knowing what constitutes ideal nutritional choices - a most excellent presentation of that knowledge is in your hands, right now. In "The Delgado Diet", Dr. Delgado has assembled the best medical and nutritional opinion, plus the fruits of his own vast experience in nutritional counseling, to create a superb, common-sense guide to optimal nutrition through healthful (and delicious!) food choices.

The guidelines presented in this book are based upon sound nutritional science and clinical experience, and reflect the growing awareness that an evolution past our current, high fat, low fiber, animal-based diet is essential if we are to create optimum health. Numerous medical studies now show that common maladies that plague our society - heart disease, high blood pressure, obesity, adult-onset diabetes, gout and other forms of inflammatory joint disease, as well as other degenerative conditions - are commonly prevented and often improved or actually cured by eating in the dietary style described in the pages to follow.

The human body has absolutely no requirement for the flesh of animals, or the milk of cows - and actually functions superbly without these cholesterol-laden, artery-clogging substances. All the protein, vitamins and other nutrients required for human health are abundantly found in the delicious grains, legumes, fruits, vegetables, seeds and other bountiful plants given to us by the Earth. This is the foundation of The Delgado Health Plan.

In "The Delgado Diet", Dr. Nick Delgado presents sound and practical advice for implementing healthful eating into a busy daily life. Far from a "diet of deprivation," the wonderful ethnic world cuisines from which these foods are prepared provide a constant parade of taste delights that are easy to make and satisfying to enjoy. "The Delgado Diet" and the life-affirming dining style it presents, is a gateway to glowing health and great eating. I recommend it most highly.

*Michael Klaper, M.D.*

# INTRODUCTION...

Wellness is about so much more than one's physical condition; true wellness is a state of mind and an entire way of living. It is a complete protocol and lifestyle approach. It is only through peak physical fitness that our bodies truly become proper vessels for mental wellbeing and spirituality. In a perfect environment, and with perfect habits, the need for supplementation is minimal. This is not the world we currently live in. Once upon a time, man foraged for sustenance from the earth's rich soil. Eating and travelling took up much of his time. Since then, human societies have advanced much further than human digestive tracts have. Our bodies still require the same large quantities of fibrous, water-bearing fruits, vegetables and superfoods that they did then, even if we no longer eat that way.

With a proper diet and by supplementing our nutritional needs throughout our adult lives, we can enjoy increased health and longevity. I've spent 35 years of my life immersed in the research and development of a unique, safe and natural diet to alleviate the biochemical imbalances and chronic diseases associated with aging. As our hormones decline from ideal levels, we grow sluggish and weary. A lifetime spent absorbing environmental toxins into our bodies also takes a toll. Then, of course, there are the poor dietary habits that plague modern man. This cookbook reflects my deepest belief . . . that nature is the best healer.

This cookbook has tasty recipes that are free of cholesterol, processed fats, low in sugar and ideally balanced in protein, essential fats, and whole superfood complex carbohydrates. These foods are high in fiber, vitamins, and minerals. Your whole family can benefit from following this nutritionally balanced plan. The utilization of this cookbook may help reduce the risk of health problems like high cholesterol, hypertension, adult-onset diabetes, hardening of the arteries, some types of cancer of the breast and colon, certain forms of arthritis and digestive disorders.

If you want fast weight loss, then select the recipes that are highest in water content and lowest in food density, such as soups, salads, fruits and vegetable dishes. As you approach your ideal weight, you will need to start eating foods that are lower in water content and higher in food density, such as gluten-free products: grains, pastas, rice, breads; beans, and sweet potatoes. Enjoy more whole soaked nuts, soaked seeds, avocados, olives and raw sprouts.

# 6 reasons for eliminating dairy, meat & oils:

- Meat and dairy contain cholesterol which clogs arteries. Even chicken, fish, turkey, egg yolk and dairy products contain as much cholesterol as red meat.

- Dairy, even non-fat dairy products, are the leading cause of food allergies.

- They are devoid of fiber, which leads to digestive problems and build up of toxins, because there isn't enough fiber to absorb poisons and harmful xenoestrogens.

- They are also more concentrated in pesticides, chemicals and hormones.

- Dairy, meat and processed oils, including "virgin olive oil", are also higher in fat than all other foods.

- Excess fats = obesity, cancer, high blood pressure, diabetes and arthritis.

*As you eat more natural foods, you will notice a need to eat a larger volume of food, along with additional in-between snacks. If you enjoy these recipes and would like to learn more about the protocol, you can continue your wellness journey by reading my other anti-aging books.*

*Here's to your health!*
*- Nick Delgado, PhD*

# TESTIMONIALS...

"I know participants truly appreciated the chance to be tested and educated about their bodies. I heard so many stories of great results after your program. They all wanted to continue their efforts!"
- Anthony Robbins

"Leading in the quest for continued longevity is Dr. Nick Delgado, who is the very epitome of virtue and a well-rounded lifestyle. Following his program will definitely improve your life."
- Dr. Bob Delmonteque

"I've been friends with Dr. Nick for many years. I've used his products and they're incredible! He's one person who knows what he's talking about. His superfoods are fantastic to use every day. I'm much healthier now and I feel more alive." - Author, John Gray

"I lost 42 lbs. in four months and I have maintained my new ideal weight for eight years. I lost all the excess fat from my hips and thighs. This is the only program that works for me because it is a way of eating well for life, and it is not a fad liquid diet. It's easy to follow the Delgado Plan for a lifetime." - Coleen Grajeda

"Most expertly presented program on health and nutrition I have ever attended. Dr Delgado, teaches and inspires one to study and practice good nutrition. His recipes in this book are terrific! Everyone should have this book for a lifetime of reference and use." - Joan Pollack

"The Delgado Plan helped me reduce my weight of 242 pounds down to 130 pounds, a loss of 112 pounds in only nine months. My cholesterol dropped from over 300 mg to 130 mg. This plan helped me to have the energy to complete the walk across America - 2,994 miles - on my hands (Bob is a double amputee) in 3½ years, ending in a meeting with President Ronald Reagan, July 7th 1986." 2012: Bob is raising America's hope at the age of 65, riding across America. DreamRide3.com
- Bob Wieland

*" To enjoy delectable, healthy, extravagantly delicious meals ALWAYS read, absorb and use "Simply Healthy" by my friend Dr. Nick Delgado.  -Mark Victor Hansen, Co-creator Chicken Soup for the Soul Series*

*"I have a great feeling of excitement and accomplishment since starting the program. I started this program right after the results of my blood test came in. The results revealed a cholesterol level of 242, exactly 100 points higher than it should be for my age. This frightened me into action because my father had just had a seven way (yes 7 way!) bypass operation and in no way was I interested in being in that position in my future. So, in earnest, I followed your program and in seven weeks my cholesterol was reduced to 144 and I feel great about it!" -Walt Herd*

*"I lost 40 lbs. I have lost six inches in the waist, going from 38 to 32; dropped my cholesterol from 205 to 130. Not one day goes by without someone coming up to me, to tell me how good I look and ask me how I did it. I had stomach problems, headaches, hurt all over my body and felt very low about myself. In just a few months, many good things have happened to me. I feel like I am 18 again, and people say I look 35. I will be 50 in January. The only thing that I regret is that I did not start this program sooner. I really did not believe this program would work. I held with this program and won. Thank You!"*
*- Richard Dolgenow*

*'The Delgado Diet' presents a rational, cultural and scientific approach to a vegan lifestyle and nutritional requirements. I have worked with serious athletes who participate vigorously, and successfully, in sports who choose the vegan lifestyle. The ones who are perennially successful supplement with the '90 for life' protocol to ensure the intake of optimal levels of all 90 essential nutrients. Dr. Delgado has joined together the wonderful culinary vegan menu, exercise and the '90 for life' supplement program to ensure the maximum level of performance, health and longevity.  -Joel D. Wallach BS, DVM, ND*

# APPETIZERS...

## Sweet-Sour Cabbage Rolls

*1 lg cabbage, cored*

### *Sauce:*

*2 onions chopped*
*1 (28 oz) can tomatoes*
*1 (8 oz) can tomato juice*
*½ c. lemon juice*
*½ c. raisins*
*¼ c. frozen apple juice*
*1 tbsp raw coconut aminos*
*¼ tsp cayenne pepper*

### *Filling:*

*½ c. cooked brown rice*
*1 tbsp raw coconut aminos*
*1 tbsp ground coriander*
*1 tsp dill weed*
*¼ tsp fennel seed, ground in blender*
*1½ c. chopped onion*
*2 c. peeled potatoes, diced med. fine*
*1½ c. chopped celery*
*½ c. chopped green bell pepper*
*2 egg whites or egg substiute, fork beaten*

Set the cabbage, cored side down, in a steamer over boiling water covered, for about 10 minutes or until leaves are soft. Let cool and separate leaves. Prepare sauce by sautéing the onions in ½ cup boiling water in a large skillet. Cook, stirring frequently, until the water has evaporated and the onions are slightly browned. Stir in the other ingredients; bring to a boil, reduce heat, and simmer (covered) for about 10 minutes.

Prepare filling by spreading rice in a baking pan and place in a 400 degree oven for about 10 minutes to toast, stirring occasionally so the rice browns evenly. Bring 2½ cups water to a boil in a saucepan. Stir in aminos, spices, and rice. Return to a boil then reduce heat to low, cover tightly, and cook for 40 to 45 minutes. Keep covered for an additional 10 minutes to allow rice to fluff from steam. Combine the rice, potatoes vegetables, and eggs, mixed well. Fill the rolls and bake in a covered dish for an hour and 15 minutes at 350 degrees. Makes 12 rolls.

# Cucumber Avocado Summer Rolls

*Juice from ½ lime*
*2 tbsp raw coconut aminos*
*1 tbsp rice vinegar*
*½ tsp Dijon mustard*
*1 tsp Stevia*
*2 avocados*
*½ English cucumber, cut into thin strips*
*2 shredded carrots*
*10 lettuce leaves*
*20 rice paper rounds*
*1 fresh bunch fresh mint*
*1 fresh bunch basil*

Stir together the lime juice, aminos, vinegar, mustard, and stevia in a bowl until dissolved and set aside. Dice the avocados into ½-inch. Dip one rice paper round into a bowl of warm water to soften then lay it flat on a towel. Dip a second round in the water and then lay in on top of the first one. Pat dry the top of the rice paper. Put a lettuce leaf on top of the two rice papers. Arrange some of the basil and mint leaves on the lettuce. Top it with a row of some of the carrot, avocado and cucumber. Lift the bottom edge of the rice paper up and roll into a tight cylinder. Fold the sides and continue to roll. Set aside and repeat with the rest of the rice paper and ingredients. This will make 10 rolls. Cut each roll in half crosswise. Makes 20 rolls.

# Grilled Sweet Potatoes

*4 sweet potatoes*
*1 tsp sea salt*
*1 tsp ground cumin*
*1 tsp paprika*
*½ tsp ground cinnamon*
*½ tsp chipotle powder*
*2 tbsp apple cider vinegar*
*¼ c. raw coconut aminos*

*Cover potatoes with cold salted water in a large pot, bring to a boil. Simmer for 7 minutes. Drain and then slice the potatoes lengthwise. Mix salt, spices and apple cider vinegar and aminos together then brush onto potatoes.*

*Grill potatoes over medium heat about 15 minutes.*

*Serves 7.*

## Raw Zucchini Boats

*2 med zucchini, cut in half lengthwise*
*¼ c. chopped green onions*
*½ c. chopped fresh tomatoes*
*1/8 tsp marjoram*
*¼ tsp pepper*
*¼ tsp basic*
*½ c. smashed, cooked garbanzo beans*

Hollow out inside of each zucchini half, leaving a ¼-inch thick shell. Chop zucchini pulp. In a medium bowl, mix zucchini pulp, green onions, tomatoes, ¼ cup of spices, and garbanzo beans. Fill zucchini halves with mixture. Place in shallow dish. Cover tightly.

Makes 4 servings.

## Zucchini Squares

*3 c. shredded zucchini*
*¾ c. all-purpose gluten-free*
 *baking flour or brown rice flour*
*2 tsp parsley*
*2 cloves garlic, minced*
*½ c. onion, chopped*
*1 tsp baking soda*
*6 egg whites or egg substitute*
*1 tsp raw coconut aminos*
*Dash of Tabasco sauce*

Preheat oven to 350 degrees. Mix aminos, Tabasco and eggs. Beat until stiff peaks form. Mix dry ingredients; blend with eggs mixture. Pour into 13 x 9 x 2-inch pan sprayed with non-stick spray. Bake 25-30 minutes until golden brown.

Makes 2-3 dozen squares.

## Stuffed Artichokes

*4 whole fresh artichokes*
*¼ c. lemon juice*
*2 peppercorns*
*4 whole cloves*
*2 slices gluten-free, rice, potato or*
  *flaxseed bread*
*1 c. chopped mushrooms*
*1 onion, diced*
*2 tbsp chopped parsley*
*½ tsp garlic powder*

Cut stem from artichokes and trim points from leaves. In a skillet, roll artichokes in lemon juice then place in a pan upright. Add about an inch of water and place peppercorns and garlic in the water. Crumble toast as fine as possible and add rest of ingredients. With a spoon, sprinkle this mixture among the leaves, use small amounts in each place. Cover and cook over a low heat for 30 minutes or until done.

Serves 4.

## Jackfruit Stuffed Tomatoes

*6 lg firm ripe tomatoes*
*½ c. green onion, chopped*
*¼ c. celery, chopped*
*2 tbsp vegetable broth*
*½ c. jackfruit, in brine*
*2/3 c. cooked brown rice*
*1 (4 oz) can mushrooms, drained*
*¼ tsp basil*
*1/8 tsp pepper*
*Dash of cayenne pepper*

Cut ¼-inch slice off top of each tomato. Scoop out pulps; drain and reserve. Place onion, celery, and vegetable broth in 1-quart casserole. Add tomato pulp, jackfruit and remaining ingredients to onion and celery. Spoon mixture into tomatoes. Place in casserole dish. Cover with plastic wrap. Bake at 350 degrees for 30 minutes. Once jackfruit is tender break it down into smaller pieces until shredded. Serve.

# Black Bean Dip

*8 oz dried black beans, cooked and drained*
*1 lg onion, chopped*
*1 jalapeño pepper, seeded and sliced*
*1 small green pepper, chopped*
*1 shallot bulb chopped*
*1 clove garlic, minced*
*1 tsp paprika*
*1 tsp dried mustard*
*3 parsley sprigs, chopped*
*Chili powder to taste*
*2 lg scallions, chopped*

Combine all ingredients in a blender, making certain that they are evenly distributed. If mixture becomes too thick while blending, add water. Refrigerate in glass or plastic containers until ready to serve.

# Cucumber Onion Dip

*1 sm avocado*
*4 tbsp dried onion*
*1 can split pea soup*
*½ tsp paprika*
*2 c. cucumber; peeled and chopped fine*
*1 tsp Worcestershire sauce*
*¼ tsp pepper*
*2 tsp lemon juice*
*½ tsp onion powder*
*Dash of Tabasco sauce*

Place avocado, split pea soup, ½ cup cucumber, pepper, onion powder, 2 tablespoons dried onion, and remaining ingredients in blender and mix until smooth. Stir in remaining cucumber and onion.

## Marinated Mushrooms

20 lg mushrooms
½ c. Italian dressing
2 tbsp fresh chopped parsley
¼ tsp raw coconut aminos
2 tbsp sherry
Garlic powder to taste
½ c. vegetable broth

Sauté mushrooms and parsley in sherry in a sauté pan for a few minutes.

Remove from heat, transfer to a bowl, add the rest of the ingredients, and marinate for

1 hour. Makes 4 servings.

## Mushroom Antipasto

1¼ c. tomato puree
¼ c. chopped fresh parsley
½ c. water
1 tsp salad herbs or Italian herb blend
2 tbsp red wine vinegar
2 tbsp apple juice
2 cloves garlic, minced
¼ tsp freshly ground nutmeg
½ green pepper, seeded and diced
1 lb sm fresh mushrooms quartered
½ red pepper, seeded and diced

Combine tomato puree and water; then combine with all other ingredients, except mushrooms, and mix thoroughly. Pour over mushrooms and marinate overnight. Serve as hors d'oeuvres or antipasto.

Makes 4 servings.

# Zucchini Noodles

*1-2 zucchini, depending on size, spiralized*
*1 c. cherry tomatoes, cut in half*
*1 red bell pepper, thinly sliced*
*¼ c. fresh basil, torn*
*¼ c. olives, roughly chopped*
*½ lemon, zested*
*1 clove garlic, thinly sliced*
*2 tsp hemp seeds*
*2 tbsp gluten free Schezwan sauce*

Toss all the ingredients together in a bowl. Drizzle in Schezwan sauce (roughly 2 tablespoons), and season with 1-2 teaspoons crystal salt and fresh black pepper.

# Collard Wraps w/Hemp Spread

*3 collard greens*
*1 avocado, sliced*
*1 tomato, cut into slices*
*1 handful of sunflower or alfalfa sprouts*

Remove stem from collard greens. Prepare Hemp Spread (see page 17). Drizzle some spread on each collard, add some veggies and sprouts, roll up, enjoy!

# Hemp Spread

*2 c. hemp seed*
*1 clove garlic*
*¼ c. pitted olives*
*¼ c. water*
*Sea salt to taste*
*Water as needed to reach*
 *desired consistency*

Place all ingredients in a
blender and blend until
smooth and creamy.

# Garbanzo Spread

*½ c. red onion, chopped*
*½ tsp cumin*
*½ bunch parsley, chopped finely*
*¼ tsp garlic powder or 2 cloves garlic*
*1 tsp basil*
*2/3 c. toasted sesame seeds (optional)*
*3 c. cooked, mashed garbanzo beans*
*Sea Salt to taste as needed (optional)*

Blend all ingredients together.

Use as vegetable or cracker dip,
sandwich spread, or with falafels.
Cook 1 cup dry garbanzo beans with
4 cups water for 3 or 4 hours.

Yield:  2 cups.

# Garbanzo Bean Hummus

½ onion, chopped
2 tbsp toasted sesame seeds
¼ c. parsley, finely chopped
1 sm clove garlic, minced
1 tbsp basil
Juice of 1 lemon
1 tbsp oregano
3 c. well-cooked garbanzo beans, mashed
2 tbsp curry powder or to taste

Sauté onions in a non-stick pan until transparent. Add a small amount of stock or water if needed to keep the onions from sticking. Add all of the other ingredients except garbanzos and sauté until parsley is soft. Add mixture to garbanzos and mix well. Serve cold as a sandwich spread or dip.

# Almond Hummus

2 c. almonds, soaked overnight, rinsed well
1/3 c. sesame seeds
2 cloves garlic
2 lemons, juiced
½ c. parsley
½ c. water
1 tbsp sea salt

Place all ingredients, except water, in a food processor and pulse until roughly ground. Use a spatula to scrape the sides, drizzle in water to reach smooth creamy consistency.

# Vegetable Hummus

½ c. finely chopped green onions
½ c. finely chopped green bell pepper
3 tbsp fresh parsley
1 tbsp Sesame Seeds
½ tsp whole oregano
½ tsp mint flakes
½ tsp garlic powder
2 c. alfalfa sprouts
1/8 tsp red pepper
1 (15 oz) can garbanzo beans, rinsed drained
4 (6-inch) gluten-free bread rounds or slices, cut in half crosswise
1 med tomato, cut into 8 (¼-inch) slices

Combine first 8 ingredients, bell pepper mixture and garbanzo beans in blender or food processor for 1 minute or until smooth. Spoon about ¼ cup bean mixture (hummus) into each bread half. Cut tomato slices in half, open sandwiches and place 2 tomato slices and ¼ cup alfalfa sprouts into sandwich half. Serve immediately. Serves 8.

## Pickled Vegetables

*2 cucumbers, thinly sliced*
*2 carrots, cut into thin strips*
*1 c. cauliflower flowerettes*
*4 sticks celery, diced*
*1 clove garlic, chopped*
*½ tsp finely chopped fresh ginger*
*1 c. fresh orange juice*
*2 tbsp vinegar*
*Freshly ground pepper*

Place cucumber, carrots, cauliflower, and celery in a serving bowl. Mix together remaining ingredients and pour over vegetables. Combine well and marinate for 1 hour before serving.

## Mock Caviar

*1 lg eggplant*
*1½ tsp lemon juice*
*1 onion, chopped fine*
*Ground pepper*
*1 clove garlic, minced*
*½ c. bell pepper, finely chopped*

Slice eggplant in half and spray each half with non-stick spray. Place halves, cut side down on baking pan. Broil on middle rack of oven for 20-25 minutes. Cool slightly, then scoop out pulp and mash with fork. Sauté onion and garlic in non-stick pan (use non-stick spray). Stir onion and garlic into eggplant pulp with remaining ingredients. Chill for 2-3 hours. Sprinkle with chopped parsley and serve with bread rounds or toast. Makes about 2½ cups.

## Potato Poppers

*¼ c. onions chopped*
*1 c. mashed potatoes*
*1 c. cooked brown rice*
*2 tbsp tomato sauce*
*1 c. toasted gluten-free bread crumbs*

Preheat oven to 350 degrees. Simmer onion in a small amount of water. Combine all ingredients and form into 1½-inch balls. Place on a non-stick baking sheet and bake until slightly browned, about 15 minutes.

## Petite Zucchini Pizzas

*4 zucchini, cut into ¼-inch thick slices*
*1/3 c. green onions, sliced*
*1½ c. mushrooms*
*1 c. organic pizza sauce*
*½ c. olives, chopped*

Arrange sliced zucchini on baking sheets. Top with 1-2 tablespoons pizza sauce, mushrooms, olives and green onions. Broil until lightly browned (4-6 minutes). Serve hot. Makes about 5 dozen.

# SAUCES, DRESSINGS & JAMS...

# Fat-Free Gravy

*6 tbsp all-purpose gluten-free baking flour
  or brown rice flour
2½ c. vegetable broth
½ tsp poultry seasoning
Pepper*

In a saucepan, whisk flour, stock, and poultry seasoning until smooth. Cook, stirring constantly, over medium heat until gravy is thickened (about 10 minutes). Season with pepper. Great on mashed potatoes.

# Mushroom Gravy

*½ onion, chopped
1 c. cooked mushroom pieces
1 tbsp arrowroot
½ tsp black pepper
1 c. water
1 tbsp vegetable broth seasoning
Dash of Tabasco
1 tbsp white wine*

In a small saucepan, sauté onion in small amount of water. Dissolve broth seasoning and arrowroot into 1 cup of water. Add mushrooms to the onions. Cook gently until thickened. Add remaining ingredients. Use on vegetables, casseroles, or stews.

Serves 4.

# Oil-Free Brown Gravy

*7 tbsp all-purpose gluten-free baking flour
  or brown rice flour
¼ tsp onion powder
1/8 tsp garlic powder
1 tsp minced dried onion
1 tbsp raw coconut aminos
2 c. cold water*

Combine flour and water. Stir until well blended. Cook over low heat until thickened, about 10 minutes. Add remaining ingredients. Continue to cook over low heat for 10 minutes, stirring occasionally. Great over vegetables, rice, or casserole dishes or stews. Makes 2 cups.

# Healthy Ketchup

*1 c. tomato paste (low-salt)
1 tbsp onion powder
3 tbsp lemon juice
1 tsp garlic powder
2 tbsp stevia
Dash red cayenne pepper or Tabasco sauce
1 tsp horseradish
1 tbsp low-sodium Dijon mustard
¼ tsp ground cloves*

Combine all ingredients, mix well and store in refrigerator.

## Cucumber Marinade

5 cucumbers, thinly sliced
1 onion, thinly sliced
1 c. red wine vinegar
1-2 tbsp honey
3 tsp dill weed
Black pepper (optional)

Place vinegar and honey in a saucepan and heat until warm. Place cucumbers, onion, dill weed, and optional pepper into a large container. Pour heated vinegar mixture over the cucumbers and onions; mix well. Cover and refrigerate at least 2 hours. Tastes even better if eaten the following day. Serves 6-8.

## Cucumber Dressing

3 lg cucumbers, peeled and cut
4 tbsp apple juice
  (frozen)
4 tbsp orange juice
  (frozen)
8 tbsp lemon juice
1 tbsp dill weed
2 cloves garlic, minced
1 tsp onion powder

Blend all until very smooth. Serves 2-4.

## French Dressing

½ c. water
2 tbsp orange juice
3 tbsp apple juice
4 tbsp lemon juice
1½ tbsp tomato puree
¼ tsp dill weed
1 tsp onion powder
1 tsp garlic powder
½ tsp paprika
1½ tsp unsweetened almond flour

Mix all ingredients, except almond flour. Mix almond flour with ½ tablespoon water, add to mix. Bring to a boil and chill. Serves 2.

## Lemon Sauce

1/3 c. all-purpose gluten-free
  baking flour or brown
  rice flour
2½ c. water
2 tbsp lemon juice
2 tbsp raw coconut aminos
½ tsp thyme
1 tsp basil
¼ tsp pepper

Toast the flour in a non-stick pan. Add the spices. Then add the liquids gradually while stirring. Simmer 5-10 minutes.

## Garlic Dressing

1 c. vinegar
½ c. water
Juice of 1 lemon
2-3 cloves garlic
½ cucumber, peeled and
seeded
Black pepper to taste

Combine all ingredients in food processor and blend for 1 minute. Place in sealed jars and store in refrigerator. Yield: 2 cups.

## French Dressing II

2 c. vegetable juice
2 c. vinegar
1 c. tomato sauce
½ c. lemon juice
3½ tbsp apple juice
¼ c. tomato paste
¼ green pepper
1 tsp celery seed
1 tsp dill weed
½ tsp paprika
¼ tsp cayenne pepper
1 tbsp arrowroot
1 onion

Combine all in saucepan. Heat to a boil and simmer 5 minutes. Cool. Chill thoroughly before serving.

## Herb Dressing I

*1 tbsp powdered fruit pectin*
*1 tsp apple juice*
*1/8 tsp dry mustard*
*1/8 tsp dried basil, crushed*
*1/8 tsp paprika*
*1/8 tsp pepper*
*¼ c. water*
*1 tbsp vinegar*
*1 small clove garlic, minced*

Combine the pectin, apple juice concentrate, mustard, basil, pepper and paprika then stir in vinegar, garlic and water. Cover and chill for 1 hour.

## Herb Dressing II

*1 c. herb vinegar*
*1 c. apple juice*
*Juice of 1 lemon*
*½ cucumber, peeled and seeded*
*2 tsp mixed herbs (parsley, chives, thyme, dill)*

Combine the first 4 ingredients in a food processor and blend for 1 minute. Add herbs but do not blend. Place in sealed jars and store in refrigerator.

Yield:  About 2 cups.

## Oil-Free Italian-Dressing

*¼ c. lemon juice*
*¼ c. cider vinegar*
*¼ c. apple juice*
*½ tsp oregano*
*½ tsp dry mustard*
*½ tsp onion powder*
*½ tsp garlic powder*
*½ tsp paprika*
*1/8 tsp thyme*
*1/8 tsp rosemary*

Combine all ingredients in blender, blend well. Refrigerate overnight or longer to allow flavors to mix. Yield: ¾ cup.

## Spicy Dressing

*1½ c. unsweetened apple juice*
*1 c. cider vinegar*
*4½ tsp garlic powder*
*4½ tsp unsweetened almond flour*
*3 tsp crushed oregano*
*1 tsp onion powder*
*1½ tsp mustard powder*
*1½ tsp paprika*
*½ tsp black pepper*

Combine all ingredients in saucepan, bring to a boil.  Cook, stirring until thickened. Chill, covered, until ready to use. Shake well before using.

Yield: about 2½ cups.

## ***Almond Tofu (used in other recipes)

1 1/3 cup boiling water
2 tablespoons agar agar
5 tablespoons stevia

1 1/3 cup almond milk
2 teaspoon almond essence

Dissolve the agar agar with boiling water, dissolve in the stevia. Add in the almond milk and essence. Pour the jelly in a shallow dish. Chill well. Enjoy!

## Sweet-Sour Vinaigrette

¾ c. water
¼ c. frozen apple juice
3 tbsp  rice vinegar
1 tbsp cider vinegar
1 tbsp lemon juice
2 tsp raw coconut aminos
2 cloves garlic, crushed
1 tbsp pectin
1 ½ tsp Arrowroot
1 tsp onion powder
½ tsp each garlic powder, paprika, and dry mustard
Dash cayenne pepper

In a small saucepan, combine all ingredients and stir to blend well. Bring to a boil, and then reduce heat and simmer, stirring constantly, until thickened (about 4 to 5 minutes).  Serve chilled or warmed.
Yield:  1 ½ cups.

## Barbecue Sauce

1 c. tomato paste (low salt)
1 tsp garlic powder
3tbsp honey or other sweetener
Dash of red cayenne pepper or Tabasco
1 tsp horseradish
1 tbsp onion powder
1 tbsp low-sodium Dijon mustard
1/4 tsp ground cloves
½ tsp liquid smoke

Combine all ingredients in jar and mix well. Store in refrigerator.

## No-Oil Raw Almond Butter

2 cups almonds, raw

Put almonds into a blender. Process for about 15 minutes scraping sides frequently.

## Sweet and Hot Chili Sauce

1½ c. seedless golden raisins
5 tbsp white vinegar
3 tsp red chili flakes
8 cloves garlic
1 tsp Sea Salt
2 fresh red chili peppers, seeded and sliced
1 c. whole canned tomatoes (with juice)
12 oz red plum jam
9 oz pineapple juice
4 tbsp apple juice

Place the first 7 ingredients in a food processor or blender and blend to an even consistency. This will take several minutes and require stopping occasionally to scrape down the sides. Place the remaining ingredients in a saucepan over medium heat. Pour the blended ingredients into the saucepan. While stirring, let this mixture come to a boil. Reduce heat to simmer and cook for 20 more minutes. Store in airtight, sterilized jars. It will keep for at least 2 months, refrigerated.

Yield: approximately 3½ cups.

## Fruity Dressing

1 cucumber, peeled and seeded
2 cloves garlic
1 c. orange juice
½ c. lemon vinegar
1 tbsp lemon rind, grated
1 tbsp orange rind, grated
2 tbsp chopped fresh herbs (parsley, basil, chives, thyme)

Combine all ingredients, except lemon and orange rinds and fresh herbs. Blend in a food processor for 1 minute. Add other ingredients but do not blend. Shake well and store in sealed jars in refrigerator.

Makes about 2 cups.

# Fruit Syrup Base

*2 pkgs frozen fruit*
*1½ c. apple juice*
*2 tbsp unsweetened almond flour*

Mix frozen fruit with unsweetened apple juice. Add almond flour; mix until blended and heat to thicken. Especially delicious with strawberries or blueberries. Other variations include peaches, apples, cherries, apricots, strawberry-banana, grape, and pineapple.

# Cranberry Sauce

*1 c. grape juice*
*2/3 c. dates*
*½ c. orange juice*
*1 (12 oz) pkg cranberries*
*½ c. apple juice*

Combine all ingredients in blender and blend for 2 minutes at high speed. Chill and serve. Makes about 3 cups

# Orange Apple Marmalade

*2 c. very thinly sliced oranges w/peels*
*3 c. dried golden delicious apples, ground*
*2½ c. apple juice*
*3 c. water*
*1 c. orange juice*

Put all ingredients in a large pot. Cook slowly about 1 hour or until oranges are tender.

## Peach Jam

*2 tbsp frozen orange juice*
*2½ c. mashed sweet peaches*
*3 tsp pectin*

Mix juice concentrate with peaches, stir in pectin and let stand 30 minutes. Stir 3 times vigorously. Serve fresh.

## Blueberry Jam

*2 c. blueberries*
*24 pitted dates (1/3 lb)*

Blend blueberries. Add dates, a few at a time. Blend until smooth. Put in jars. May be kept up to 3 days if refrigerated. Other jams can be made, substituting other fruit for the blueberries: strawberries, peaches, apples, etc.

Makes 1 pound or 1½ cups.

## Peach / Apricot Jam

*3 c. diced peaches or apricots*
*1½ tsp lemon juice*
*1½ tsp agar-agar*
*2 tbsp apple juice*

Cover and cook peaches or apricots in a saucepan without added water for 10 minutes over low heat. Remove the lid and bring the juice to a boil for 1 minute. Then remove from heat. Soften agar-agar in lemon juice for 5 minutes. Pour some of the hot fruit juice from the fruit into the agar-agar mixture and stir until completely mixed and dissolved. Stir mixture into the fruit. Add 2 tablespoons apple juice. Allow to cool and store in the refrigerator.

# BEVERAGES...

## The Dr. Delgado Daily Superfood Nitric Oxide Monster

This ultimate smoothie is rich in nutrients, phytochemicals, and live raw enzymes, (including Protein Plus, Stem Cell Strong and Slim Blend powders which are kept under 118 degrees). It is rich in natural nitrates to produce nitric oxide. It is also high in raw cruciferous vegetables with DIM & I3C to detoxify harmful estrogens and high in cleansing fiber & protein. Rich in vitamins and minerals, this smoothie is low in extracted fats and high in omega fatty acids. This is Nick's typical morning breakfast prior to his strength endurance workout. For this recipe you will need both a blender (Vitamix is preferred) and a juicer.

### Blend:
*1 beet*
*1 handful napa cabbage*
*1 bok choy*
*1 handful Kale*
*1/2 lime*
*1 banana*
*1 scoop Slim Blend Detoxifying Superfood*
*1 scoop Stem Cell Strong powder*
*1 scoop Delgado Protein Plus*
*Ice to taste*
*Add 3 c. of juice recipe on right*
*(Use coconut water if juicer is not available)*

### Add to juicer:
*8 large peeled carrots*
*4 swiss chard leaves*
*4 kale leaves*
*14 leaves of assorted greens*
*1 bunch of wheatgrass*

Start by making juice in juicer. Then add all vegetables, and juice contents to blender. Make sure that there is enough liquid to cover vegetables. Blend entire mixture. Serve cold.

Serves 2 (48 ounces total).

## Mom's Vegetable Drink

*2 c. kale (about 4 large leaves – remove stems)*
*1 c. Swiss chard (about one large leaf – remove stem)*
*½ c. fresh beets, chop and peel*
*\*Include one leaf with stem from beet*
*½ c. fresh spinach*
*1 tbsp Slim Blend powder*
*1 over-ripe large banana to sweeten*
  *(or appropriate frozen or fresh fruit)*
*¾ c. 100% pomegranate juice*
*1¼ c. water*

Wash ingredients thoroughly and pack into a blender. Variation: in the event one of the above ingredients is lacking you can use these as follows: arugula, bok choy (baby or regular), Chinese cabbage aka Napa cabbage, parsley, romaine lettuce, carrots, raw sweet potatoes. Makes approximately 5 cups.

## Carob Chai Tea

*½ c. cold water*
*½ c. almond milk*
*1/3 c. carob powder*
*2 tsp dry chai powder*
*2 c. boiling water*

Place the cold water, rice milk, carob powder, and chai powder in a blender. Blend until the dry ingredients dissolve. Add the boiling water and blend at high speed for about 30 seconds or until mixture becomes frothy and all the ingredients are well blended. Serve immediately.

Makes 2 servings.

## Strawberry Juice

*2 tbsp arrowroot*
*2 tbsp tahini*
*2 tbsp coconut nectar*
*2 c. fresh strawberries*
*2 tsp vanilla*

Combine ingredients in a saucepan. Blend in arrowroot. Cook until thickened, stirring constantly. Place in blender and mix. Pour mixture into a shallow tray and freeze for 1-2 hours until edges are firm but center is still slushy. Stir well and return to the freezer until firm. Process in food processor or beat with an electric mixer until smooth. Serves 8.

# Pina Colada Smoothie

*1 c. pineapple chunks*
*1 c. unsweetened coconut milk*
*1 banana*
*¼ c. ice cubes*
*2 tsp coconut nectar*
*Garnish: pineapple wedges*

Combine the pineapple chunks, banana, ice, coconut milk and nectar. Puree until smooth. Makes 2 servings. Garnish with a pineapple wedge.

# Papaya Ginger Smoothie

*2 c. ripe papaya chunks*
*1 c. coconut milk yogurt*
*1-inch piece of ginger, chopped*
*1-2 tbsp coconut nectar*
*Few fresh mint leaves*
*2 fresh lemons, juiced*
*Few ice cubes*

Blend all ingredients. Pour in a glass. Garnish with mint leaves. Serve chilled.

# Refreshing Raspberry Mojito

*1½ c. frozen or fresh raspberries*
*½ English cucumber, sliced*
*1 sm bunch of mint leaves*
*Purified water*
*2-3 tbsp of Stevia*
*A pitcher for serving*
*Ice cubes*

Combine raspberries, cucumber, and mint in a blender. Lightly puree the mixture with 1-2 cups of water and ice. Pour into a pitcher; add a few whole mint leaves and raspberries. Stir in a little more water, stevia, and ice cubes.

# Green Smoothie

*1 banana, roughly chopped*
*4 or 5 strawberries*
*½ c. fresh blueberries*
*1 small peach, peeled and roughly chopped*
*1 heaping c. (or more) fresh spinach leaves, thoroughly rinsed*
*1 tbsp coconut milk yogurt*
*2 tsp coconut nectar*
*½ c. crushed ice*

Place all ingredients in a blender and blend until smooth.
Serve immediately. Serves 2.

# Raspberry Banana Avocado Smoothie

*1 c. frozen raspberries*
*1 avocado*
*1 frozen banana, optional\**
*1 c. coconut milk yogurt*
*Stevia*

*Peel and cut the bananas into chunks (5-6 or even small
pieces if you're in a hurry). Place in a baggie and freeze.

Blend all ingredients in your blender or food processor.
Add sweetener to taste. Yields one large serving or two
smaller ones.

# Cinnamon Apple Smoothie

*1 apple, chopped*
*¾-inch slice almond tofu*
*¼ c. unsweetened apple juice*
*¾ c. unsweetened almond milk*
*1 c. raw spinach*
*½ tsp cinnamon*

Place all ingredients in a blender and blend until smooth.

# Peachy Lychee Lime Smoothie

*1-2/3 c. unpasteurized fruit juice, your choice:*
  *(best bets - orange, pineapple, peach or guava juices)*
*6 whole lychees, frozen*
*¾ c. frozen peaches*
*1 lg frozen banana*
*1 lime, squeezed*
*¾ c. ice cubes (plain water or coconut water)*
*¼ c. lychee juice ice cubes (frozen from can liquid)*

Optional add-in: handful of fresh strawberries. Or a handful shredded raw coconut. Garnish: lychee or peach fruit – or a lime wedge. Packed with healthy fruit, this blended beverage will provide you with antioxidants, fiber, vitamin C, vitamin A and plenty of potassium.

Serves 2.

## Chocolate Banana
## Sweet Potato Smoothie

*12 oz of almond milk , chocolate flavor*
*½ banana*
*½ c. cooked sweet potato*
*3 tbsp unsweetened cocoa powder*
*1 tbsp almond butter*
*½ tsp of cinnamon*
*About 1 c. of ice*

Add all ingredients together in blender with ice and blend until very thick.

## Green Tea Spirulina Frapp

*8 oz of almond milk*
   *(green tree flavor recommended)*
*2 tbsp of green tea powder*
*1 tsp of Stem Cell Strong powder*
*1 tsp spirulina*
*1 c. of ice*

Add all ingredients together in blender with ice and blend until very thick.

## Raw Acai Lift

*1-2 c. of kale or spinach*
*½ packet of frozen acai*
*5 strawberries or handful or blueberries*
*½ banana*
*8 oz unsweetened almond milk*
*1 c. of ice*

Variation: for more vegetables and added protein, add ½ cup of a cucumber and 2 stalks of celery, or 2 beets. Add all ingredients together in blender with ice and blend until very thick.

## Pumpkin Spice
## Yam Smoothie

*1/3 c. yam or sweet potato*
*1/3 c. organic pumpkin mix*
*8 oz almond milk*
   *(vanilla flavor recommended)*
*Dash of cloves*
*Dash of nutmeg or pumpkin pie seasoning*
*1 tsp cinnamon*
*1-2 medjool dates, seeded (optional)*
*About 1 c. of ice*

Add all ingredients together in blender with ice and blend until very thick.

## Orange Julius Energizer

¼ *of an orange*
*1 sm banana*
*½ c. orange juice*
  *(optional if using more whole oranges)*
*¾ c. of fresh cashew milk (or other vanilla nut milk)*
*1 big handful of fresh spinach (or other leafy greens)*
*1-2 medjool dates, seeded*
*A few cubes of ice*

Puree all ingredients in a blender, add more nut milk or water, if needed, until smooth.

## Blueberry Bliss

*1/3 c. frozen organic blueberries*
*1 sm banana*
*1 sm handful of fresh mint*
*1 handful of fresh spinach*
*1 c. of fresh cashew milk (or other vanilla nut milk)*
*1-2 medjool dates, seeded*
*1-2 tbsp hemp seeds*
*A few cubes of ice*

Puree all ingredients in a blender, add more nut milk or water, if needed, until smooth and creamy.

## Antioxidant Elixir

*1/3 c. frozen organic blueberries*
*½ frozen acai smoothie packet*
*½ banana*
*¾ c. unsweetened almond milk*
*1 handful of fresh kale*
*1 stalk of celery*
*1-2 medjool dates, seeded*
*About ½ c. of ice*

Puree all ingredients in a blender, add more nut milk or water if needed until smooth.

## Fresh Cashew Milk

*About 1 c. whole raw cashews*
*About 1 tsp vanilla bean or extract*
*About 1 tsp Stevia or Xylitol (optional)*

Soak raw cashews overnight, or for 4 hours or more, until they are soft. Drain the water. Use a blender to liquefy the cashews adding a little water at a time until you get a smooth and milky texture. Add a small amount of vanilla and sweetener. Make sure the end product is blended very well and is not too thick or too thin.

# Chilled Tropical Smoothie

*4 1/2 cups unsweetened coconut milk*
*10 cups unsweetened almond milk*
*3 bananas*
*2 ripe mangoes*
*2 ripe papayas*
*30 dates*
*1 lb roasted macadamia nuts*

Pour the coconut milk into two ice cube trays after shaking the cans to mix them. Put the ice cube trays in the freezer. Remove the date pits. Cut the bananas, mangoes and papayas into cubes. Place all of the ingredients, into plastic bags and place in the freezer, until frozen solid. Keep the almond milk refrigerated. For each serving, place in the blender: 3 coconut milk cubes, 3 dates, 1 cup of almond milk, 2 papaya chunks, 2 mango chunks, ¼ cup macadamia nuts, 1 banana chunk. Puree together until it has a smooth and thick consistency.

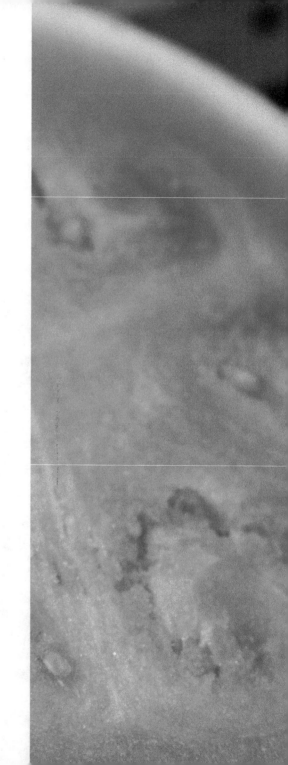

# Watermelon Frosty

*2¼ c. frozen watermelon cubes*
*½ c. water*
*2 tbsp Stevia or Xylitol*
*1 lg lemon, squeezed*
*1 fresh banana*

Add all ingredients into blender. Blend until smooth. Garnish with watermelon slice. Enjoy!

Serves 2.

# Banana Oatmeal Smoothie

*2 whole bananas*
*2 c. ice*
*1/3 c. coconut milk yogurt*
*½ c. cooked gluten free oatmeal*
*1/3 c. almonds*

Add all ingredients into blender. Blend until smooth. Serves 2.

# Energy Almond Shake

*2 c. almond milk, vanilla flavor*
*2 lg frozen bananas, ripe*
*2 tbsp almond butter*
*½ c. ice*
*¼ tsp cinnamon*
*Roasted almonds*

Place all ingredients in a high power blender. Blend on high until smooth and thick. Pour into glasses and garnish with roasted almonds.

# Ginger Cleanser

*1-2 tbsp fresh ginger juice*
*4 oranges*
*1 tbsp honey*
*½-1 tsp cayenne*

Using a citrus juicer, juice the oranges with pulp. Place into a blender with the ginger, cayenne, and honey and blend.

# Hot Tea Immunity

*2 c. reishi tea*
*1 tbsp Slim Blend powder*
*1 tbsp coconut water*
*1 tbsp Stem Cell Strong powder*
*1 tsp vanilla powder*
*1 tsp Stevia*

Place all ingredients into a blender and blend on high for 45 seconds to 1 minute.

## Superfood Icee

*20 oz blended ice cubes*
*1 scoop Stem Cell Strong powder*
*½ tsp vanilla powder*
*1 squirt Stevia*
*4 tbsp unsweetened almond milk*

Blend all ingredients until smooth.
Serve chilled.

## Slim Blend Colada

*1 scoop Slim Blend powder*
*4 oz chopped pineapple*
*1/8 tsp cinnamon*
*1/8 tsp nutmeg*
*1 tbsp coconut nectar*

Blend and serve.

## Coconut Protein Cleanse

*2/3 c. coconut water*
*2/3 c. ice*
*3 tbsp water*
*1 tbsp lemon juice*
*1 tbsp Delgado Protein Plus*
*2 drops trace minerals*
*1 tbsp ginger*
*1/2 tsp sea salt*
*½ tsp vanilla*
*1 tsp Stevia*

Blend all ingredients together until smooth.

## Cinnamon Cider

*1 tbsp cacao powder*
*1 c coconut water*
*1 scoop Stem Cell Strong powder*
*2 tbsp Cinnamon*
*1 tsp coconut nectar*

Blend and serve.

## Tropical Superfood Latte

*2 tbsp coconut flakes*
*1 tbsp of goji berries*
*14 oz. pineapple*
*1 scoop Stem Cell Strong powder*
*4 c. water*
*1 tbsp coconut water*
*1 tbsp Slim Blend powder*
*Pinch of sea salt*
*1 tsp Stevia*

Simmer the coconut flakes, water and goji berries for 30 minutes. Add all ingredients to a blender. Blend until smooth and serve.

## Fruit Shake

*2 peeled oranges*
*2 peeled bananas*
*2 c. crushed ice*
*1½ c. apple juice*
*Dash of cinnamon*

Blend in blender (add ice gradually). Sprinkle cinnamon on top.

## Cranberry Delight

*4 c. cranberry juice, chilled*
*1 tbsp lemon juice*
*1 egg white or egg substiute*
*½ c. crushed ice*

Blend all ingredients until foamy. Serve immediately. Serves 2.

## Strawberry Shake

*4 c. orange juice, chilled*
*2 c. frozen strawberries*
*½ tsp almond extract*

Blend all ingredients in blender and serve cold. Serves 4.

# Cranberry Tea Punch

*5 herbal tea bags or 5 tsp loose tea*
*¼ tsp ground cinnamon*
*¼ tsp ground nutmeg*
*2½ c. boiling water*
*2 c. cranberry juice*
*1½ c. water*
*½ c. orange juice*
*1/3 c. lemon juice*

Boil tea in water, slowly stir in nutmeg and cinnamon. Cook 3 mins then mix in liquid ingredients.

# Cranberry Spritzer

*3 c. cranberry juice, chilled*
*1 c. unsweetened pineapple juice, chilled*
*Lime slices (optional)*
*33 oz sparkling water*
*½ c. lemon juice chilled or orange juice, chilled*

Mix all juices. Garnish with lime.

# Orange Delight

*1 c. fresh orange juice*
*1 banana*
*1 tsp coconut nectar (optional)*
*1 c. fresh apple juice*
*1 c. crushed ice*
*Shake of cinnamon*

Blend at high speed until frothy. Serves 2-3.

## Cranberry Glog

*1 (40 oz) bottle cranberry-apple juice*
*½ c. raisins*
*½ c. cranberries*
*½ tsp cardamom (optional)*
*4 oranges, each studded with 2 whole cloves*
*½ tsp or 1 stick cinnamon*

Combine all ingredients in a medium sauce-pan. Bring to a boil. Simmer for 30 minutes. Let stand 1 hour. Serve hot in mugs. Serves 6.

## Harvest Punch

*1 gal unpasteurized apple juice*
*4-8 whole cloves*
*4 tsp allspice*
*6 cinnamon sticks*
*1 c. orange juice*
*Dash coconut nectar (optional)*
*Juice of 1 lemon*

Bring all ingredients to a slow boil and simmer about 10 minutes. Strain and serve hot. Serves 20.

## Peach Spritzer

*2 (21 oz) cans peach nectar, chilled*
*1 c. unsweetened orange juice, chilled*
*½ c. lemon juice, chilled*
*Crushed ice*
*33 oz sparkling water*
*Orange slices (optional)*

Combine juices together in a large pitcher, stirring well. Pour ½ cup mixture over crushed ice in a tall glass; add ½ cup sparkling water. Repeat for each serving; garnish with orange slices, if desired.

## Lemon Cooler

*4 c. fresh apple juice*
*½ c. lemon juice*
*Lemon wedges for garnish*
*2 tbsp frozen pineapple juice*

Place all ingredients in blender and process for 2 minutes. Serve ice cold and garnish with lemon wedges. Serves 4.

## Carrot-Apple Juice

*2 oz fresh apple juice*
*2 oz fresh carrot juice*
*1 sm apple, coarsely chopped*
*3 ice cubes*

*Combine in blender and liquefy.*
Serves 1.

## Pineapple-Cucumber Juice

*3 oz cucumber, peeled*
*1 oz fresh pineapple*
*3 ice cubes*
*½ fresh apple, coarsely chopped*
*2 parsley springs*

Combine in blender and liquefy.
Serves 1.

## Tomato Juice

*4 c. fresh tomato juice*
*4 long stems of green onions*

Trim and wash stems.
Sip juice through stem.

# SALADS...

Most of you who know me personally know I eat a mammoth raw kale salad almost every day. Not only is kale delicious but it is among the greatest of **super foods**.[1] One cup of kale contains 36 calories, 5 grams of fiber, and 15% of the daily requirement of **calcium** and **vitamin B6** (pyridoxine), 40% of magnesium, 180% of **vitamin A**, 200% of **vitamin C**, and 1,020% of **vitamin K**. It is also a good source of minerals copper, potassium, iron, manganese, and **phosphorus**. Its health benefits are primarily linked to the high concentration of antioxidant **vitamins A, C, and K** — and sulphur-containing **phytonutrients**. Additionally, it[1] contains specific types of antioxidants associated with many of the **anti-cancer** health benefits. Kale is also rich in the eye-health promoting lutein and **zeaxanthin** compounds. The **fiber** content of[1] kale binds bile acids and helps lower blood cholesterol levels and reduce the risk of heart disease. This salad is also rich in **probiotics**.

1. Chicago: The Truth About Kale: Nutrition, Recipe Ideas, and More, http://www. webmd.com/food-recipes/features/the-truth-about-kale (accessed January 6, 2013)

## Nick Delgado's Daily Kale Salad

*3 c. kale*
*2 c. spinach and arugula*
*½ avocado*
*1 c. shredded carrots*
*1 c. chopped shiitake mushrooms*
*½ c. celery*
*½ c. cucumbers*
*½ c. cranberries*
*½ c. eggplant*
*½ c. tomatoes*
*½ c. broccoli*
*¼ c. chopped red onions*
*¼ c. green onions*
*¼ c. green, red and yellow peppers*
*¼ c. raw organic cultured kraut*
*1 daikon radish*
*8 oz organic hearts of palm*
*6 asparagus heads*
*1 oz organic capers*
*7 tbsp lemon juice or cut and squeeze a half of a lemon*
*6 sprays raw coconut aminos*
*½ c. Live Food sprouted hummus*
*Pinch of sea salt*
*Pepper, to taste*

Put the kale into a salad bowl. Mix the ingredients together. Add lemon juice and seasoning.

**Enjoy !!**

# Dragon Fruit, Pomegranate and Macadamia Nut Salad

## *Salad:*

*4 c. fresh greens,*
*1 dragon fruit, skin removed and diced*
*Seeds of 1 fresh pomegranate*
*½ c. raw macadamia nuts*
*1 avocado, sliced*

Add all of the ingredients to one large bowl and toss. Serve with dressing on the side or tossed.

## *Dressing:*

*¼ c. rice or balsamic vinegar*
*Juice and zest of one fresh lime*
*½ c lemon juice*
*½ avocado*
*5 sprigs fresh mint*
*6 drops liquid Stevia*
*Pinch sea salt*
*2-3 tbsp filtered water for consistency*

Add all of the ingredients in a blender and puree until smooth.

# Quinoa Almond Berry Salad

*¾ c. dry quinoa*
*3 c. strawberries, sliced*
*2 c. fresh blueberries*
*1 c. cherries, pitted and sliced*
*6 drops liquid Stevia*
*1 tsp balsamic vinegar*
*1 tbsp fresh lime juice*
*Pinch of sea salt*
*½ c. almonds, chopped*


Cook the quinoa. Slice the fruit and put into a large bowl. Add in the quinoa once ready. Mix together the dressing ingredients. Mix in the dressing.

Serves 5.

# Avocado Mango and Macadamia Salad

*1 lg mango, cubed*
*1 avocado, diced*
*¾ c. macadamia nuts, roasted/salted*
*5 c. fresh arugula*
*Sweet onions*
*Diced apple*
*Diced pineapple*

## *Dressing:*

*¼ c. lemon juice*
*2 tbsp apple cider vinegar*
*1 tbsp Dijon mustard*
*3 drops liquid Stevia*
*Pepper*
*Dash garlic powder*

Whisk together the dressing ingredients and toss it with the salad ingredients - except the arugula! Toss the avocado, mango and nuts with the salad dressing - then pour it over the greens. Top with fresh black pepper! Serve!

# Summer Salad

*1 lg yellow peach*
*1 heirloom tomato*
*1 c. cherries, halved and pitted*
*2 tbsp basil*
*2 tbsp cilantro, chopped*
*1 tbsp mint, chopped*
*1 tbsp lime juice*
*1 tbsp coconut nectar or 3 drops liquid Stevia*
*3 tbsp rice or balsamic vinegar*
*Sea salt and pepper, to taste*

Cube the tomato, slice up the peach and combine with the cherries in a large bowl. Add the basil, cilantro and mint. Whisk or blend the sweetener, lime juice, vinegar, salt and pepper until mixed together. Pour the dressing in the bowl & enjoy.

Serves 2 - 4.

# Shaved Asparagus and White Bean Salad

*2 bunches fresh asparagus*
*1 tbsp raw coconut aminos*
*1 med red onion, thinly sliced*
*3½ c. cooked cannellini beans*
*2 tbsp fresh orange juice*
*1 tbsp champagne vinegar*
*2 tbsp fresh lemon juice*
*½ c. chopped unsalted walnuts*
*¼ c. slivered basil*
*Sea salt and black pepper, to taste*

Shave the asparagus into long ribbons. Place ribbons in a large bowl and drizzle with liquid aminos. Add in orange and lemon juices, beans, onion and vinegar. Toss. Add walnuts and basil. Sprinkle in salt and pepper.

# Thai Mango Salad

*1 yellow Thai mango*
*1 zucchini*
*1 cucumber*
*2/3 c. snap peas*
*Fresh coriander*
*Fresh mint*
*2 tbsp tamarind juice*
*1 lime*
*1 tsp coconut nectar or 3 drops liquid Stevia*
*Sea salt*

Slice the mint, coriander, snow peas and mango. Make cucumber ribbons and zucchini using a spiralizer. For the dressing, mix salt, sweetener, lime and tamarind juice. Toss all of the ingredients including the dressing and serve.

Serves 2.

## Quinoa with Nectarines and Pistachios

*1 c. quinoa*
*½ tsp Dijon mustard*
*¼ tsp ground black pepper*
*¼ tsp sea salt*
*2 tbsp vegetable broth*
*2 diced nectarines*
*1 bunch sliced watercress*
*1 tbsp apple cider vinegar*
*½ c. pistachios, chopped*
*¼ c. thinly sliced shallot*

Boil 1½ cups of water to a boil in a saucepan. Stir the quinoa into the saucepan. Cover the pan and remove from heat. In a bowl, whisk together mustard, vinegar, vegetable broth, salt and pepper. Add quinoa, watercress, pistachios, nectarines, and shallots to bowl and toss to combine. Serve warm or chilled.

Serves 4.

# Spicy Stir-Fried Tofu with Kale and Red Pepper

*1 bunch curly kale (about 10 oz), stemmed and washed*
*14 oz almond tofu, sliced about ¼-inch thick*
*1 tbsp raw coconut aminos*
*1 tbsp shao hsing rice wine or dry sherry*
*¼ c. vegetable stock*
*¼ tsp tsp sea salt*
*¼-½ tsp ground white pepper*
*¼ tsp Stevia*
*1 tbsp rice or balsamic vinegar*
*1 tbsp minced garlic*
*1 tbsp minced ginger*
*1 serrano pepper, seeded and minced*
*1 red bell pepper, cut in 2-inch julienne*

Bring a saucepan with salted water to a boil. Add the kale and cook for about 1 minute. Drain excess water. Then chop the kale and place in a bowl nearby. Cut the tofu into cubes and place it between paper towels to drain excess fluids. Combine the rice wine or sherry, aminos, and stock. Combine the stevia, pepper and salt in another bowl. Heat a wok or skillet over high heat. Add in vinegar, then the tofu. Cook for 1-2 minutes. Add the ginger, chili and garlic and stir-fry for 10 seconds. Add the red pepper and cook for 1 minute. Add the stevia, pepper and salt mixture along with the kale and toss together. Add amino mixture. Cook for another minute. Remove from heat and serve with healthy grains such as brown rice or quinoa.

Serves 4.

# Grilled Peach Arugula Salad

*6 peaches, cut in half and pitted*
*Sea salt*
*3-4 lg handfuls arugula, washed & dried*
*1 sm red onion, slivered*
*½ c. white balsamic vinegar*
*2 tsp. honey*
*2 tsp. whole-grain mustard*
*2 tbsp minced chives*

Light a grill until it is medium hot. Drizzle the peaches with 1/3 cup vinegar, lightly salt and then place them on the grill. The peaches are done once they are soft and charred. Whisk honey, chives, mustard and 4 tbsp vinegar in a bowl adding white balsamic vinegar to taste. Toss in the remaining ingredients. Sprinkle with sea salt. Serve.

# Cucumber Salad

*3 med cucumbers*
*1 clove garlic, chopped*
*1 tsp finely chopped fresh ginger*
*2 tsp freshly ground  black pepper*
*1 tbsp toasted sesame seeds*
*1 tbsp raw coconut aminos*
*½ c. fresh orange juice*
*2 tsp vinegar*

Peel cucumbers and slice into thin discs. Mix with other ingredients, except sesame seeds. Marinate for 30 minutes before serving. Toss in sesame seeds and serve.

# Crunchy Beet Slaw

*3 med beets, peeled and grated*
*1 med carrot, grated*
*1/3 jicama, diced*
*½ tsp Dijon mustard*
*2 tbsp orange juice*
*2 tbsp lemon juice*
*Peel of 1 orange, finely grated*

In a salad bowl, combine beets and grated carrot. In another bowl, stir together orange peel, mustard and juices. Dress slaw and chill briefly before serving. Serves 4.

## Sprout Salad

2 c mixed sprouts (lentils, azuki, etc.)
3-4 green onions, sliced
1 stalk celery, sliced
2.2 oz jar chopped pimentos
1 c. sliced mushrooms
3 or 4 tbsp chopped fresh coriander
   or parsley

### Dressing:
2 tsp Dijon mustard
1 tbsp water
2 tbsp white wine vinegar
1 tsp Worcestershire sauce
1 tbsp raw coconut aminos
¼ tsp black pepper

Mix salad ingredients in large bowl. Place the mustard and the water in a small bowl and mix well. Add remaining ingredients and mix, then pour over the sprout salad. Toss to coat. Refrigerate before serving.

## Brocco-Bean Salad

1 bunch broccoli
1 can red kidney beans, rinsed
3 tbsp Mrs. Pickford's (no-oil) vinaigrette
   dressing or equivalent
Dash of Mrs. Dash
Dash of salad herbs
4 green onions, chopped

Steam broccoli (cut up) for 8 minutes, cool slightly. Combine all ingredients and refrigerate ½ hour (or more) before serving.

## Chunky Avocado Salad

3 avocados, diced
1 sm carrot, coin cut
½ c. purple cabbage, chopped
1 clove garlic, minced
2 tbsp hemp seeds
3 tbsp fresh parsley, chopped
1 tsp chipotle powder
½ lemon, juiced
2 tbsp coconut water
2 tsp crystal salt
2 tsp fresh black pepper

Add all ingredients to a large bowl and gently toss together. This is a great topper on fresh cucumbers, beets or carrots slices.

# Summer Fruit Salad

¼ *watermelon*
½ *cantaloupe*
½ *honeydew melon*
1 *lb seedless grapes*
2 *c. strawberries*
2 *c. raspberries*
2 *c. cherries*
2 *c. blueberries*

Remove rind from the melons. Slice melons into wedges. Stem grapes. Hull strawberries. Pile strawberries in the center of a large basket or tray; surround with melon wedges, raspberries and cherries. Garnish with grapes and blueberries. Serves 8 to 10.

# Alfalfa Sprout Salad

3 *stalks celery,*
  *diagonally sliced*
1 *cucumber, peeled and sliced*
6 *shallots, cut diagonally*
1 *tbsp chives*
1 *red apple, cored and*
  *cut into strips*
2 *tomatoes, chopped*
1 *c. alfalfa sprouts*
1 *tbsp parsley*
10 *button mushrooms,*
  *thinly sliced*

Combine all ingredients and squeeze lemon juice over them. Toss lightly and serve in lettuce cups or on a bed of shredded lettuce. Serves 2.

# Orange Coleslaw

½ *head cabbage*
2 *oranges, segmented*
½ *c. green pepper, thinly sliced*
½ *c. red pepper, thinly sliced*
½ *tsp grated lemon rind*
2 *tsp orange rind*

Combine all ingredients and let stand for 1 hour. Toss lightly and chill for 2 hours before serving. Serves 2.

## Dressing:

2 *tbsp orange juice*
2 *tbsp lemon juice*
1 *tbsp vinegar*
*Black pepper, to taste*

Combine all and toss over coleslaw before serving. Serves 2.

# Carrot Salad

*¼ c. walnut pieces*
*1 tbsp shredded coconut*
*2 c. grated carrot*
*½ c. orange juice*
*Zest and juice of ½ lemon*
*1 apple, cored and grated*
*½ c. currants*
*sea salt*
*1½ tsp grated fresh ginger*

Toast walnut pieces and coconut in a low 300 degree oven. The walnuts will take about 10 minutes and the coconut 5 minutes. Chill. Combine grated carrots, apple, lemon zest, orange, and lemon juices, currants, sea salt, and ginger. Add walnuts and coconut and serve.

Makes 3 cups. Serves 4.

## Finocchio Salad

1½ c. brown rice noodles
½ c. sliced fennel
¼ c. chopped Italian parsley
¼ c. diced bell pepper
1 c. sliced raw mushrooms
2 tbsp chopped chives
1/3 c. sliced black olives
2-3 tbsp lemon juice
2 tbsp no-oil Italian dressing
½ tsp Sea Salt
Freshly ground black pepper

Cook macaroni until tender in salted, boiling water. Cool and combine with fennel, parsley, bell pepper, mushrooms, chives and olives. Mix 2 tablespoons lemon juice, salt and pepper. Toss salad in dressing: taste and add remaining tablespoon of lemon juice, if desired. Makes 5½ cups.

## Polynesian Fruit Salad

1 lg pineapple
1 c. peeled, seeded, diced papaya
1 mango peeled, pitted, and diced
1 banana, sliced
1 c. strawberries, sliced
½ c. lychees
½ c. shredded coconut

Halve pineapple lengthwise through crown. Cut out fruit, leaving a ¼-inch shell. Remove core; dice fruit and place in large bowl. To pineapple, add other ingredients. Mix lightly. Spoon fruit into pineapple shells. Sprinkle with coconut.

## Mushroom and Walnut Salad

*4 c. romaine/butter lettuce*
*10 cherry tomatoes, halved*
*½ lb mushrooms, sliced*
*2/3 c. walnut pieces*
*2 green onions, sliced*
*2 tsp dijon mustard*
*1/8 tsp pepper*
*1/8 tsp paprika*
*2 tsp dry basil leaves*
*5 tsp white wine vinegar*

Whisk together the vinegar, mustard, paprika, basil and pepper in a large bowl until blended. Add in the green onions and mushrooms. Chill for 30 minutes. Top with tomatoes, lettuce and walnuts. Toss.

Serves 4.

## Quinoa Tabouli

*1 c. quinoa*
*8 scallions, chopped*
*¼ c. finely chopped parsley*
*¼ c. chopped fresh mint*
*3 ripe tomatoes, chopped*
*¼ c. lemon juice*
*¼ tsp black pepper*

Bring 2 cups of water to a boil; add quinoa. Cook for 45 minutes. Place quinoa in a bowl with water to cover. Allow to soak 15 minutes, then drain and squeeze dry. Mix all ingredients and serve on lettuce leaves, chopped vegetables or gluten-free crackers.

## Sweet Potato Oatmeal Breakfast Casserole

½ c. gluten free oats
2 c. organic almond milk
1 lg ripe banana
1 sm sweet potato, peeled, chopped
1 tbsp chia seeds
1 tsp ground cinnamon
1/8 tsp nutmeg
1-2 tsp pure vanilla extract
¼ tsp sea salt
2 tbsp pure liquid Stevia

## Crunchy Pecan Topping:

1/3 c. chopped pecans
2 tbsp almond butter
2 tbsp spelt flout
¼ c. Stevia

 Set oven to 350. Boil 3 cups of water in a pot and add in the sweet potato chopped and peeled. Cook for 5 minutes over medium heat. Drain and set aside. Add chia seeds, oats and milk to a pot. Bring to a boil while whisking. Cook on low heat for 5-7 minutes while stirring. Once finished, mash in banana and sweet potato. Stir in the sea salt, vanilla, nutmeg, 2 tbsp stevia and cinnamon. Cook for 3 minutes. For the topping, mix together the stevia, almond butter, flour and pecans. Spread the oatmeal mixture evenly in a 8 in casserole dish then sprinkle on the pecan topping. Bake for 20 minutes. Then set your oven to broil for a few minutes to lightly char the topping.

 Serves 4.

## Fat Metabolizer Breakfast Bowl

*½ c. goji berries,*
  *soaked 20 min, strained*
*¼ c. hemp seeds*
*2 tsp chia seeds*
*¼ c. coconut flakes*
*2 tsp maca root*
*½ tsp holy basil*
*2 tbsp coconut water*
*½ tsp Stevia leaf*

Mix all ingredients well in a bowl and serve.

## Cinnamon Prune Sticks

*1 box pitted prunes*
*1 c. spicy apple cider*
*2 cinnamon sticks*

In a medium saucepan, empty the box of prunes, add cider and cinnamon sticks. Simmer on low for 30 minutes. Enjoy these spiced prunes hot or cold. Makes 8-10 servings.

## Tropical Muesli

*5 c. rolled oats*
*1-1/3 c. flaked coconut*
*4 oz banana chips*
*¾ c. Brazil nut pieces*
*4 oz candied pineapple*
*1 c. bran*

Mix all ingredients together making sure they are evenly distributed. Store in large screw-top jar. Yield about 6 cups

## OrangeCoco Granola

*3½ c. old-fashioned rolled oats*
*1 c. chopped walnuts*
*1 c. shredded coconut*
*1 c. chopped almonds*
*½ c. sesame seeds*
*1 tsp cinnamon*
*½ tsp ground cloves*
*¼ c. honey*
*2 tbsp grated orange peel*
*½ c. dried apricots*
*½ c. raisins*

Combine all ingredients. Spread mixture in 2 large baking pans. Bake uncovered, at 200 degrees for 55 minutes. Cool completely and then stir in ½ cup raisins and ½ cup chopped dried apricots. Cover and store at room temperature. Makes 8 cups.

## Breakfast Potatoes

*15 sm red potatoes, cubed*
*1 med onion, chopped*
*1 red bell pepper, chopped*
*½ green bell pepper, chopped*
*1 tbsp garlic powder*
*1 tbsp onion powder*
*¼ tsp black pepper*
*½ tbsp oregano*
*½-1 c. water*

Place ½ cup water in non-stick skillet and heat. Add potatoes and cook for about 5 minutes. Add remaining ingredients and simmer until tender.

## Power Breakfast

*½ c. goji berries,*
  *soaked 20 min, strained*
*¼ c. hemp seeds*
*2 tbsp chia seeds*
*¼ c. coconut flakes*
*2 tsp Stem Cell Strong*
*1 tsp mesquite powder*
*½ tsp sea salt*

Mix all ingredients well in a bowl and serve.

## Sweet Potato Pancakes

*2 lb sweet potatoes, peeled
  and cut into 1-inch pieces*
*1 c .minced onions*
*2 tbsp almond flour*
*1 c. egg whites or substitute*
*Pepper to taste*
*Applesauce, unsweetened*

Finely chop potatoes in processor until pulpy. Do not puree. Transfer to large bowl. Mix in onions. Let stand about 10 minutes. Drain potatoes and onions through fine sieve, pressing down to extract all liquid. Stir 2 tablespoons flour and egg into potato mixture. Season with pepper. Form into patties and place in non-stick skillet. Cook until potatoes are brown, 1-1½ minutes. Turn and cook until the other side is brown. Serve with applesauce. Makes 12 pancakes.

## Herb Pancakes

*¾ c. gluten-free flour*
*1/4 tsp baking powder*
*½ c. water*
*3 tbsp almond butter*
*1 c. egg whites or egg substitute*
*1 tbsp minced fresh basil*
*1½ tsp minced fresh thyme*
*1½ tsp minced fresh rosemary*
*1½ tsp minced fresh sage*

Mix all ingredients together. Heat non-stick griddle or skillet. Ladle batter onto griddle. Cook until bottom side is brown, about 2 minutes. Flip over. Makes 1 dozen pancakes.

## Zucchini Pancakes

*3 c. shredded zucchini*
*1/3 c. minced onion*
*6 egg whites or egg substitute*
*¾ c. all-purpose gluten-free baking flour
  or brown rice flour*
*¾ tsp Rumford baking powder*
*¼ tsp pepper*
*½ tsp oregano leaves*
*Grated vegan cheese (optional)*

Blend all ingredients, except vegan cheese. In a non-stick skillet, spoon about 3 tablespoons of the zucchini mixture for each pancake. Cook 4 pancakes at a time, turning once, until golden brown on each side. Sprinkle the vegan cheese. Makes 4 servings.

# Fluffy Vegan Fruit & Honey Pancakes

*¼ c. almond flour*
*¼ c. gluten-free oats*
*1 tsp Rumford baking powder*
*½ c. coconut milk*
*½ c. egg substitute*
*½ tsp vanilla*
*1 pinch of sea salt*
*2 tsp coconut nectar*
*Your favorite soft fruit*
*Honey*

Set oven to 350. Whisk ¼ "egg" until fluffy. Meanwhile in another bowl mix vanilla, honey, salt, flour and the other ¼ cup "egg". Then add in warm coconut milk. Add in the remaining "egg". Sprinkle the pan with lemon juice. Cook the batter until the edges are set. Add in fruit on top. Oven bake until golden, about 7 minutes. Top off with coconut nectar. Serves 1.

# French Toast

*4 slices gluten-free bread*
*1 c. apple juice*
*1 tbsp tapioca granules*
*½ tsp cinnamon*
*½ tsp vanilla*
*1 tbsp date pieces*
*1 ripe banana*

In this order, add the apple juice, tapioca, cinnamon, vanilla, dates, and banana into a blender and blend for 3 mins. Dip the bread into the mixture and bake on a griddle sprinkled with lemon juice until browned. Serve with fruit spread. Serves 4.

# French Raisin Toast

*2 slices gluten-free raisin bread or*
  *gluten-free waffles*
*2 egg whites or egg substitute*
*1 tsp vanilla extract*
*½ tsp cinnamon*
*½ tbsp apple juice*

In a shallow bowl, beat eggs together with other ingredients. Dip both sides of bread in batter until soaked with mixture. Spray griddle with non-stick spray; brown on both sides. Serve with fruit topping and/or apple butter.

# Easy Blueberry Sauce

*2 c. apple or mixed berry juice*
*1 (10 oz) jar blueberry preserves*
*2-3 tsp kudzu or arrowroot*
*½ c. cold water*
*Pinch sea salt*
*Pinch cinnamon or nutmeg*
*1 tsp vanilla*
*1 pt blueberries (fresh or frozen)*
*1-2 tsp lemon juice (optional)*

This sauce is a perfect replacement for the butter and maple syrup that usually top pancakes. It is also delicious on cake instead of fat, dense frosting.

Pour juice into a saucepan and slowly bring to a boil. Add blueberry preserves and continue to simmer. Dissolve kudzu or arrowroot in cold water and add to simmering sauce. Stir until the sauce thickens and becomes clear and shiny. Stir in salt, cinnamon, or nutmeg and vanilla. Add blueberries and lemon juice, if desired. Stir. Lower flame and keep warm until ready to serve. Serves 8.

# Cocoa Almond Butter Banana Spice Oatmeal

*½ c. gluten free rolled oats*
*1 tbsp of almond butter*
*½ banana*
*2 tbsp unsweetned cocoa powder*
*1 tsp cinnamon*
*1 c. almond milk*

Mash ½ banana. In a saucepan on the stove, boil milk or water and banana with cocoa, almond butter and spices. Slowly pour in oats and stir. Simmer for about 10 minutes or until thick and serve. Serves 1.

# Vegan Lemon Poppy Seed Quinoa Pancakes

*½ c.  brown rice flour*
*½ c. quinoa flour*
*2 tbsp Stevia*
*1 tsp Rumford baking powder*
*½ tsp baking soda*
*2 pinches sea salt*
*2 tbsp poppy seeds*
*Finely grated zest of 1 lemon*
*½ c. egg substitute*
*1 c. coconut milk*
*For PANCAKE MIX: 1 tsp lemon juice*
*FOR FRYING PAN: 1 tbsp lemon juice*
*plus more for cooking pancakes*

Add 1 pinch of salt, stevia, baking powder & soda, quinoa & rice four, lemon zest and poppy seeds to a bowl. Meanwhile in another bowl whisk together 1 pinch of salt, lemon juice, coconut milk and the "egg". Add the dry ingredients to the "egg" mixture and stir well. In a saucepan heat 1 tbsp of lemon juice. Pour ¼ batter for each pancake into the saucepan and repeat. Cook the pancake until the edges are set then flip and cook for 2 more minutes. Serve with honey or blueberry sauce (pg 77). Garnish with lemon zest.

# Vegetarian Omelette

*12 egg whites or egg substitute*
*½ c. salsa*
*1 c. cauliflower, sliced*
*½ lb Italian green beans*
*1 pkg frozen or fresh chopped spinach, thawed*
*8 oz almond tofu*
*½ tsp basil*
*½ tsp oregano*
*½ tsp Veg-It seasoning*
*1 onion, chopped*
*2 cloves garlic, minced*
*¼ lb mushrooms*

Steam fresh beans and cauliflower over boiling water until crisp tender (4-5 minutes). Cut tofu into ¾-inch cubes. Heat water to saute in a frying pan over medium heat. Add onion, garlic, and mushrooms; cook until onion is soft. Add beans, cauliflower, spinach; basil, oregano and Veg-It seasoning. Cook until heated through. Add eggs. Add tofu. Cook until eggs are set. Pour salsa on top.

## Berry Oat Omelette

*4-6 egg whites or egg substitute*
*3 tbsp water or almond milk*
*½ c. strawberries or blueberries*
*½ banana, chopped or mashed*
*¼ c. gluten free oatmeal*
*Non-stick spray*

Cook oatmeal. Beat eggs, water or milk until eggs are stiff. Add blueberries to mix and mash in. Spray browning skillet with non-stick spray. Pour omelette mixture into skillet. Cook on medium high for 3½ minutes or until knife inserted in center comes out clean. Spread half of the strawberries and the banana to the omelette. Fold omelette over and spread remaining strawberries over top before serving.

Variation: use ½ banana instead of other fruit mashed in omelette. Then add 2 tablespoons of unsweetned cocoa powder to egg mixture.

## Crepes

*1 c. all-purpose gluten-free baking flour*
  *or brown rice flour*
*1½ c. apple juice*
*4 egg whites or egg substitute, stiffly beaten*
*1 tbsp apple juice*

Blend eggs with 1 1/2 cups apple juice. Then add 1 tbsp apple juice and blend in the flour. Pour 1/3 cup batter into heated non-stick pan. Brown crepe on both sides to golden. Note: crepes may be served alone or with fruit or other toppings.

## Omelette

*1 sm tomato, diced*
*½ yellow onion, chopped*
*1 zucchini, sliced and quartered*
*3 oz fresh mushrooms, sliced*
*¼ c. green bell pepper, chopped*
*2 tbsp chili salsa*
*6 egg whites or egg substitute, beaten*
*4 slices rice, potato or flaxseed gluten-free*
*toast  Dash of pepper to taste*

In a non-stick skillet, sauté first 5 ingredients. Add salsa and pepper. While mixture simmers, pour eggs into pan, stirring while it cooks to keep from sticking. Cook until eggs are set. Spoon over toast. Serves 2 to 3.

# Huevos Rancheros I

*1 steamed brown rice tortilla*
*1 egg white or egg substitute, poached*
*¼ c. green chilies*
*¼ c. salsa*

Top steamed tortilla with poached egg, chilies, and salsa. Makes 1 serving. Variation: You may also add ½ c cooked beans (vegetarian whole beans).

# Huevos Rancheros II

*2 brown rice tortillas*
*3 egg whites or egg substitute*
**Sauce:**
*2 lg onions*
*1 green bell pepper*
*1 (14 oz) can tomatoes*
*1 (14 oz) can vegetable broth*
**Garnish:**
*½ c. salsa*
*Fresh cilantro*
*Chopped green onion*
*2 thin slices of avocado*
*2 slices low-fat or shredded vegan cheese*

Place 1-2 cooked tortillas on a plate. Scramble eggs and place on top of tortillas. Add ½ cup salsa and garnish with fresh cilantro, chopped green onions, avocado and vegan non-dairy cheese. To prepare sauce: in a frying pan, sauté onions and green pepper in a little water until soft. Add tomatoes and broth. Boil, uncovered, stirring to prevent any sticking, until sauce is reduced to about 2½ cups.

# Sunrise Patties

*12 egg whites or egg substitute*
*8 oz almond tofu*
*1 stalk celery, chopped*
*1 green onion, chopped*
*½ c. zucchini, shredded*
*1/8 lb mushrooms, sliced*
*¼ lb bean sprouts*
*Pepper*
*1 tsp sherry*

In a large bowl add in sherry and almond tofu for 5 minutes. Add in all remaining ingredients. Heat a large frying pan over medium heat. Use ¼ cup mixture for each patty and 2 tablespoons "egg" over the top of each patty. Cook until set and gold brown.

## Apricot Breakfast Bars

½ c. apple juice
1 banana
¼ c. egg substitute
½ tsp lemon juice
1 tsp vanilla extract
½ tsp cinnamon
½ c. pitted dates
4 pitted apricots
½ c. gluten free oat bran

In a blender mix together apple juice, banana, "egg", lemon, cinnamon, and oat bran. Pour into a baking dish. Bake for 30 minutes at 350. Meanwhile blend the vanilla, apricots and dates in a blender. After 30 minutes top the bars with the apricot mixture and bake for 10 mins at 400. Serves 4.

## Buckwheat Breakfast Pudding

1 c. cooked buckwheat
¼ c. unfiltered apple juice
½ c. diced apples
1/8 tsp nutmeg
¼ tsp cinnamon
½ tsp vanilla
3 tbsp raisins
1 tbsp chopped walnuts

Mix all ingredients together and bake in a non-stick pan for 30 minutes at 350 degrees. Serves 2.

## Breakfast Cherry Cobbler

3 c. frozen cherries (unsweetened)
¾ c. gluten free oats
½ c. granola
½ c. chopped walnuts or pecans
6 oz cherry cider or apple cider
½ tsp pure vanilla extract
½ tsp cinnamon

Spread cherries on the bottom of a glass 8x10 baking dish. For the topping, combine oats, granola, nuts and cinnamon and sprinkle over the cherries. Whisk together vanilla and cider and pour on top. Bake for 30 minutes at 350.

## Banana Bread

*1½ c. gluten-free flour*
*¼ c. gluten free oat bran*
*1 tsp cinnamon*
*2 tsp Rumford baking powder*
*½ tsp baking soda*
*½ c. chopped nuts*
*¼ c. almond butter*
*½ c. honey*
*¾ c. vanilla*
*1 c. mashed banana*
*1 c. egg substitute*

Preheat oven to 350 degrees. Combine dry ingredients, including nuts. Combine wet ingredients and stir into dry mixture until thoroughly blended. This will make a thick batter. Spread in a floured 8½ x 4-inch loaf pan. Bake for 45-50 minutes or until a toothpick inserted comes out clean. After cooling for 10 minutes in the pan, transfer to a cooling rack. Allow banana bread to cool completely before cutting. Note: for any bread recipe that calls for oil, just replace oil with the equivalent volume of applesauce and water.

## Banana Bread II

*1 pkg. Fearn gluten-free banana cake mix*
  *(available in health food stores)*
*1 pkg. almond butter*
*½ c. honey*
*2 mashed bananas*
*2 egg whites or egg substitute*
*1/3 c. rice milk*
*1 c. walnuts, chopped*

Preheat oven to 350 degrees. Mix almond butter and honey. Add bananas and eggs; mix again. Add contents of cake mix and rice milk alternately, ending with mix. Add nuts and stir until uniform. Turn into a 1-pound loaf pan. Bake for 60 minutes. After 30 minutes, loosely place a sheet of foil over top of bread to prevent crust from browning excessively.

## Carrot Bread

*1 c. all-purpose gluten-free baking flour*
  *or brown rice flour*
*1 c. gluten free oat bran*
*1 tsp baking soda*
*2 tsp Rumford baking powder*
*1 tsp cinnamon*
*¼ tsp nutmeg*
*4 egg whites*
*2 c. grated carrots*
*1 tbsp almond butter*
*1/3-½ c. pineapple juice*
*½-1 c. raisins*

Combine all ingredients and mix well. Bake in non-stick loaf pan at 325 degrees for 45 minutes.

## Almond Bread

*1 1/4 c. almond flour*
*1/2 c. coconut flour*
*1/4 c. ground chia seeds*
*5 egg whites or egg substitute*
*1/4 Tsp sea salt*
*4 raw coconut aminos*
*1 Tbsp apple cider vinegar*
*1/2 tsp baking soda*

 Mix all ingredients together well. Pour into a loaf pan. Bake for 45 mins at 350 degrees.

## Pumpkin Bread

*1/3 c. almond butter*
*½ c. orange juice*
*4 egg whites or egg substitute*
*1 c. can organic pumpkin mix*
*1 tsp baking soda*
*1 tsp cinnamon*
*½ tsp nutmeg*
*1/8 tsp ginger*
*1¾ c. all-purpose gluten-free baking flour*
  *or brown rice flour*

In a blender, process almond butter, juice, and eggs. While blending, add pumpkin, baking soda, cinnamon, nutmeg and ginger. Gradually add flour until you get a doughy consistency. Bake in a non-stick loaf pan (use non-stick spray) in a pre-heated 350 degree oven for 45-60 minutes. Toothpick should come out clean when done.  Makes 1 loaf.

# Zucchini Bread

3 c. all-purpose gluten-free baking flour
  or brown rice flour
3 c. grated zucchini
1¼ c. gluten free oat bran
4½ tsp Rumford baking powder
1 tsp nutmeg
2 tsp cinnamon
1 c. chopped nuts
4 egg whites or egg substitute
1¾ c. applesauce
2 tsp vanilla extract

Preheat oven to 350 degrees. Mix together the flour, oat bran, baking powder, nutmeg, cinnamon, and nuts. In another bowl, mix the eggs, applesauce, and vanilla extract. Stir in the grated zucchini. Add the flour mixture to the zucchini mixture; gradually stirring until blended. Turn the batter into 2 (8½ x 4½-inch) loaf pans and bake.

# Sweet Potato Bread

1 c. mashed sweet potato, cooled
½ c. frozen apple juice
1 tbsp unsweetened almond milk
4 c. gluten-free flour
¼ tsp nutmeg
1 tbsp cinnamon
1 tbsp raw coconut aminos
¾ c. water

In a blender, process the spices, aminos, apple juice, rice milk and potato until smooth. Transfer to a bowl and add in 3 ¼ cup flour. Mix together well. Knead adding in the rest of the flour. Put into a loaf pan. Bake for 10 minutes at 425. Brush with almond milk. Then bake at 375 for 40 minutes. Cool & slice.

# Apple Almond Muffins

¾ c. all-purpose gluten-free baking
  flour or brown rice flour
2/3 c. unsweetened almond flour
1 tsp gluten free baking flour
1 apple, finely grated
2 stiffly beaten egg whites
½ c. unfiltered apple juice
¼ c. pureed dates or date powder

Blend all ingredients together, mix
well. Pour into non-stick muffin pan
2/3-full and bake in 350 degree pre-
heated oven for 15-20 minutes or until
done. Makes 8 muffins.

# Sweet Cornbread Muffins

1½ c. yellow whole-grain cornmeal
1 tsp baking soda
1 egg white or egg substitute
½ c. millet (optional)
¾ c. unsweetened applesauce
3 tbsp unfiltered apple juice
1 c. rice milk

In a large bowl, combine all ingredients
and mix well. Pour into non-stick muffin
pan 2/3-full and bake in 350 degree pre-
heated oven for 15-20 minutes or until
done. Makes 8 muffins.

*Note: Corn is a common allergen. We recom-
mend a delayed food allergy test before trying
this recipe.*

# Pumpkin Muffins

¾ c. organic canned pumpkin mix
4 egg whites or egg substitute
½ c. coconut nectar
½ c. apple juice
1½ c. gluten-free baking flour or rice flour
1 tsp pumpkin pie spice
¾ tsp Rumford baking powder
½ tsp baking soda
½ c. walnuts, chopped
½ c. raisins

Combine pumpkin, eggs, honey, apple juice.
Add to combined dry ingredients in large bowl.
Mix until blended. Stir in nuts, raisins. Spoon 2
tablespoons batter into ceramic muffin molds.
Bake: 425 degrees, 15-20 minutes.

# Prune Muffins

1 c apple juice
1 egg substitute
1 t cinnamon
1 c pitted prunes
1 c grated zucchini
1 c gluten free oatmeal

In blender, combine first 4 ingredients. In a
bowl, combine rest of ingredients with blender
mixture. Pour into non-stick muffin pans; bake
at 350 degrees, 30 minutes. Makes 12.

# Bran Muffins

*2 egg whites or egg substitute, beaten*
*1 c. apple juice*
*½ c. all-purpose gluten-free baking flour or brown rice flour*
*1 c. gluten free oat bran*
*3 tsp cinnamon*
*1½ tsp Rumford baking powder*
*1 tsp ground cloves*
*grated orange peel*
*½ c. unsweetened pineapple*
*¼ c. chopped pecans or walnuts*
*¼ c. raisins*

Mix all dry ingredients. Add raisins, nuts and spices; mix well. Add orange rind, apple juice and egg whites. Bake at 400 degrees for about 25 minutes. Makes 12 muffins.

# Oat Bran Muffins

*2 egg whites or egg substitute*
*1 c. apple juice*
*1 c. gluten-free pancake mix*
*1 c. oat bran*
*2 tsp cinnamon*
*½ c. unsweetened crushed pineapple*
*¼ c. chopped pecans or almonds*

Beat the eggs in a bowl with a mixer. Mix in the apple juice. In a separate bowl mix the pancake mix, oat bran, and cinnamon. Mix dry and liquid ingredients together until well blended. Do not beat. Add the crushed pineapple and pecans. Divide into 12 equal-size muffins. Bake in a non-stick muffin pan at 400 degrees for 15 minutes.

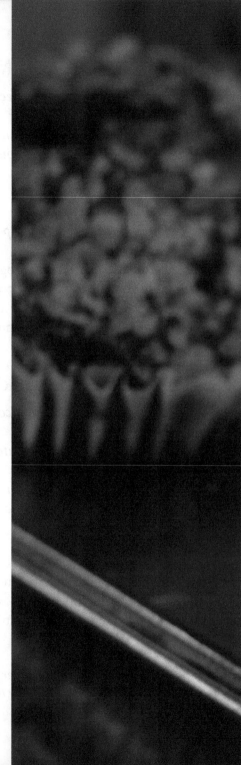

# MAIN DISHES...

## Eggplant Italian

*1 eggplant, sliced ½-1-inch thick (do not peel)*
*1 jar your preferred spaghetti sauce*
*1 tsp garlic powder*
*gluten free bread crumbs*
*mushrooms*

Place some of the eggplant in the bottom of baking dish. Cover with some of the spaghetti sauce and sprinkle some of the garlic powder and mushrooms over sauce. Continue this layering process until pan is full. Sprinkle a coating of gluten free bread crumbs on top. Bake in oven at 350 degrees for about 1 hour, or until eggplant is tender.

# Fettuccine with Tomatoes and Wild Mushrooms

*1 c. tomato sauce*
*¼ c. minced shallots*
*6 oz fresh mushrooms, chopped*
*6 tomatoes, sliced*
*white pepper, to taste*
*1 lb whole wheat fettuccine or gluten-free fettuccine*
*2-3 green onions, sliced*

Sauté shallots dry, stirring 1 minute over medium heat. Add mushrooms and tomatoes and stir 3 minutes. Season with pepper. Cook fettuccine in a large pot of boiling water until tender. Drain well. Transfer to a large bowl. Add mushrooms and tomatoes. Garnish with green onions and serve.

# Italian Potato Casserole

*5 lg. potatoes*
*1 lg. onion, sliced*
*4 c. fresh green beans*
*1 (28 oz) can pureed tomatoes*
*2 cloves garlic, pressed*
*2 tsp Italian seasoning*
*Freshly ground pepper*

Chop potatoes into large chunks and place in large casserole dish with onion and green beans. Mix pureed tomatoes with garlic and seasoning; pour over vegetables. Add ground pepper if desired. Bake at 350 degrees for approximately 1 ½ hours. Check potatoes with a fork for softness. Makes 4 to 6 servings.

# Homemade Marinara Sauce

5 tomatoes, chopped
2 (15 oz) cans tomato sauce
1 can tomato paste
1 onion, chopped
3 cloves garlic, minced
1 sm bell pepper, diced
12 mushrooms, sliced
2 carrots, sliced
2 sm zucchini, sliced
2 bay leaves
1 tsp black pepper
½ tbsp basil
½ tbsp oregano
¼ tsp sage
¼ c. red cooking wine

Add all the ingredients together (except for the dry herbs) into a large pot on the stove. Simmer for about 2 hours. Add the dry herbs and simmer for another 1 to 2 hours. Use sauce on spaghetti, in lasagna, or with any other Italian dishes.

# Italian Eggplant Spaghetti

4 oz  brown rice spaghetti
1 lg. eggplant, peeled
   and cut into cubes
1 med. carrot, chopped
1 med. onion, chopped
1 (6 oz) can tomato paste
1 (4 ½ oz) can tomatoes
1 tsp dried basil, crushed
½ tsp pepper
1 ½ tsp dried oregano, crushed
2 cloves garlic, minced
1 sm. zucchini, chopped

Cook spaghetti accordingly and drain. Steam zucchini, carrot, onion and eggplant until crisp and tender.  In a large bowl stir together pepper, oregano, basil, garlic, undrained tomatoes and paste with the steamed vegetables. In a 12x 7 baking dish spread 2 cups of the tomato mixtures on the bottom. Top with spaghetti and then layer with remaining tomato mixture. Bake for 35 minutes at 350.

Serves 6.

# Lasagna

*Gluten-free lasagna noodles (9-10 12-inch strips)*
*1 med zucchini, sliced thin*
*¾ c. frozen green peas*
*½ sm eggplant, peeled and cut in half*
  *or quarters, sliced thin*

## Sauce:

*½ med onion, chopped*
*1 stalk celery, chopped*
*1 carrot, grated*
*½ green pepper, chopped*
*½ c. fresh mushrooms, chopped*
*1 (28 oz) can crushed tomatoes with added puree*
*½ tsp basil*
*1 tsp oregano*
*½ tsp thyme*
*½ tsp marjoram*
*½ tsp onion powder*
*2 tbsp fresh parsley*

Spread a little sauce on the bottom of a shallow rectangular baking dish, 8 x 11-½ inches. Cover with a third of the noodles. Spread one-half of the zucchini, egg-plant, and peas over the noodles. Then spread with sauce. Repeat the layers. Cover with remaining noodles and sauce. Cover and bake for 45 minutes at 350 degrees. Remove the cover and bake for 10-15 minutes. Sauté onion in ½ cup water. Add celery, carrots, green peppers, and mushrooms and cook 5 minutes. Add herbs and onion powder. Then add the tomatoes.

Simmer 10-15 minutes.

## Spinach Lasagna

*8 oz uncooked brown rice lasagna noodles*
*1 eggplant, thinly sliced into rounds*
*1 lg bunch fresh spinach with stems removed*
*1 tsp oregano*
*1½ c. fresh mushrooms, sliced*
*1 onion, chopped*
*1 c. organic spaghetti sauce (no-oil)*

Cook noodles, remove from water immediately, and separate. Spray 9 x 14-inch baking dish with non-stick cooking spray. Layer first with noodles, then with eggplant. Spread 4 teaspoons of sauce over this. Layer again with noodles and top with remaining sauce, mushrooms and onion. Cover and bake at 350 degrees for 45 minutes. Cut into squares after allowing cooling. To serve, layer 2 squares together for thickness. Serves 4.

# Beetballs (Vegan, Gluten-Free Sausage)

1/2 ounce dried porcini mushrooms
1 medium raw beet
1/2 cup raw pecans, almonds, or other nuts
1/2 medium red or yellow onion, chopped
2 cloves garlic, chopped
1 cup cooked chickpeas
2 tablespoons ground flax seeds
2 teaspoons oregano

¼ tsp red pepper flakes
¼ tsp freshly ground black pepper
¼ tsp hickory smoked salt
   or liquid smoke (optional)
1 tsp smoked paprika (mild or spicy)
1 tsp sea salt
½ tsp rubbed sage
¼ – ½ tsp fennel seeds

Boil the mushrooms in 1 cup of water in a saucepan and simmer for 10 minutes. Remove, rinse and set aside. Save 1 tbsp of the mushroom broth. Meanwhile pulse the nuts in a blender until chopped fine. Set aside. Peel and cube the beet. Add the beets, mushrooms, chickpeas, onion and garlic in a blender and pulse until chopped. Mix the nuts and chopped vegetables in a large bowl with 1 tbsp mushroom broth. Set the oven to 350. Use your hands to form 1 tbsp of dough into compact balls. Put on a cookie sheet and bake for 35 mins until crisp and brown.

Serves 4.

# Spaghetti Squash

*1 c organic spaghetti sauce*
*1 spaghetti squash*
*1 c grated zucchini*
*1/8 t basil leaves*
*1/2 cup red onion, chopped*
*1 cup black beans, rinsed and drained*
*2 teaspoons vegetable broth*
*1/2 cup red pepper, chopped*
*1 jalapeño chili, seeded, minced*
*1 teaspoon chili powder*
*1 tablespoon lime juice*
*1/3 cup cilantro, minced*
*1 teaspoon sea salt*
*Dash of garlic powder*

Set oven to 375. Cook for 50 mins. Once cool, scoop out filling. Save the shell. In a saucepan, sauté red pepper, jalapeno, and onion in vegetable broth for 2 mins. Add chili powder and beans. Saute 1 min. Add salt, lime juice, cilantro and squash filling. Cook 1 more minute. Fill squash shell. Serve.

# Spaghetti Squash II

*½ spaghetti squash*
*1 c. organic spaghetti sauce*
*¼ tsp pepper*
*1/8 tsp basil leaves*
*1 c. grated zucchini*
*Dash of garlic powder*

Cut squash in half lengthwise and clean out seeds. Place squash, cut side down, in a pot with 2 inches of water. Cover and boil for 20 minutes. If you are using a microwave, place squash, cut side up, in a dish with ¼ cup water. Cover and cook 7-8 minutes. Run fork over inside of cooked squash to get spaghetti-like strands.

Scoop out spaghetti from ½ cooked squash. Add the other ingredients. Mix well and spoon back into the empty squash. Sprinkle on 2 tablespoons grated vegan parmesan cheese, bake at 350 degrees for 20 minutes.

The squash will separate into spaghetti-like lengths and have the texture of firm, cooked spaghetti.

It has only 66 calories in an 8-ounce serving.

# Pasta Primavera

½ c. peas
½ c. diced carrots
½ c. zucchini
1 c. broccoli flowerettes, broken in small pieces
1 lg onion diced (1 c.)
1 pkg gluten-free brown rice noodles (2 c.) cooked
2 tsp unsweetened almond flour
1 c. vegetable stock

Steam the vegetables until crisp-tender and set aside. Bring the water to a boil. Add the pasta, return to a boil. And cook 8-10 minutes or until it has a slight resiliency (al dente). While the pasta is cooking, combine the vegetable stock and almond flour and stir until the almond flour is complete dissolved. Bring to a boil. Reduce the heat and simmer stirring constantly, until thickened; set aside. Drain the pasta thoroughly and put it in a large bowl. Pour the thickened vegetable stock over the pasta and toss thoroughly. Add the steamed vegetables and again toss thoroughly. Divide into 4 servings (1¾-cup each).

# Pasta La Mer

2 c. cooked gluten-free macaroni
¼ c. chopped celery
¼ c. frozen green peas (or fresh)
¼ c. diced green or red bell pepper
1 tbsp vinegar
1 tsp low-sodium Dijon mustard
Juice from 1 lemon
1 c. bean sprouts
¼ c. chopped green onions

Toss all ingredients together in a bowl. Chill before serving. Serves 4.

# Steamed Kale and Coconut Quinoa Almond Tofu

### Sweet Chili Almond Tofu:
*14 oz almond tofu*
*1 tsp vegetable broth*
*3 cloves garlic, minced*
*1 tbsp fresh ginger, grated*
*½ tsp chili flakes*
*2 tbsp coconut nectar or 6 drops liquid Stevia*
*2 tbsp raw coconut aminos*
*1 tbsp lime juice*

### Coconut Quinoa:
*1 tbsp ginger, grated*
*3/4 c. quinoa*
*1 c. coconut milk*
*½ c.water*
*4 cardamom pods, crushed*
*¼ tsp sea salt*

### Steamed Kale:
*1 bunch kale, stems removed, washed, chopped*
*1-2 tbsp water*
*1 tsp raw coconut aminos*
*1 tsp lime juice*
*2 green onions, chopped*
*½ c. almonds*

## Directions:

Combine the quinoa, ginger, coconut milk, water, cardamom & sea salt in a pot and bring to a bowl. Cover and cook on low heat for 20 mins. Let sit and steam for 10 minutes with lid. Dry tofu and cut into cubes. Saute the almond tofu cubes in vegetable broth until browned on each side. Add in chili, ginger and garlic and sauté for 5 mins. Add in the lime juice, 2 tbsp aminos and sweetener. Cover and cook until liquid is gone then add in the chopped kale, lime juice, 1 tbsp aminos and water. Saute the kale for 4 mins. Place the quinoa in a bowl. Add the kale, tofu, green onions, almond and lime slice. Serve.

# Tomatoless Spaghetti Sauce

*4 carrots, sliced*
*4 stalks celery, sliced*
*1 green pepper, diced*
*½ c. beets , diced*
*1 c. warm water*

Dice the beets. Steam the beets, celery, carrots, green pepper, and warm water for 20 minutes, or until tender.

Heat a pan and sauté:
*3 cloves garlic, minced*
*2 lg onions, chopped*
*¼ c. water*
*Non-stick spray*

**Add to vegetables and mash or puree in blender.**

Dissolve:
*3 tsp sesame paste*
*½ c. warm water*

Add to vegetables with:
*½ c. warm water*
*2 tbsp coconut aminos*
*2 tbsp mirin*
*1 tsp oregano*
*1 tsp basil*
*Pinch of cayenne*

Steam the green pepper, carrots, celery and beets for 20 minutes in warm water. Dissolve 3 tsp dark miso and ½ cup warm water in a saucepan. Add this to the steamed vegetables. Add in a pinch of cayenne, 1 tsp basil, 1 tsp oregano and 1/c warm water. Meanwhile in a saucepan sauté 3 minced garlic cloves, 2 chopped onions, ¼ cup water. Once sautéed, put the sauce and steamed vegetables in a blender. Serve with noodles.

# Eggplant & Pepper Caponata

*1 sm eggplant*
*1 red pepper or 1 (4 oz) jar pimento peppers*
  *or roasted peppers*
*¼ c. salt-free tomato juice*
*2 cloves garlic, minced*
*¼ c. onion, finely chopped*
*1 stalk celery, finely chopped*
*2 tbsp sweet basil*
*¼ tsp cayenne pepper or crushed red pepper*
*¼ tbsp red wine vinegar*

With sharp knife, pierce whole eggplant several times and place whole into baking dish. Cut red pepper in half, discard seeds. Place in pan with eggplant. Place in broiler, several inches away from fire, and broil 10 minutes or until eggplant and peppers are soft and charred on one side. May also be baked in 450 degree oven. Bake an additional 10 minutes until soft and charred.

In bowl or food processor, place the remaining ingredients, the eggplant, and peppers and any liquid from cooking. Process or mash with a fork until ingredients are blended but still chunky. Chill 1 hour before serving. Serve as a vegetable dip or on bread or crackers.

Makes 2 cups.

# Broiled Red Pepper and Eggplant Antipasto

*1 round sm firm purple eggplant*
*½ tsp granulated garlic*
*2 tbsp minced sweet basil*
*1 lg red bell pepper*

Cut eggplant into 2-inch strips lengthwise. Seed and cut red pepper into quarters. Prepare baking sheet by lightly spraying with lemon juice. Place eggplant and peppers on baking sheet and sprinkle with spices. Place the backing sheet into the broiler close to the flame. Broil until browned. This can also be grilled on a barbecue.

Serves 4.

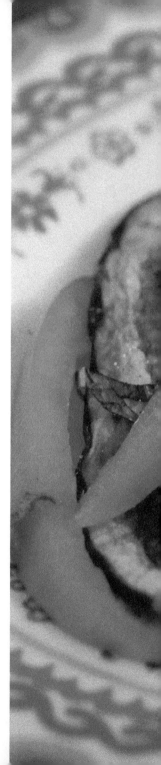

# Gluten & Yeast Free Vegetarian Pizza

1½ c. warm water
2 tsp dry basil
2 tsp oregano
¼ c. gluten free oat bran
1½ c. brown rice flour
almond flour for kneading
1 (14 oz) can artichoke hearts, quartered
1 lg red onion
1 (15 oz) can tomato sauce
1 (6 oz) can tomato paste
2 zucchini, thinly sliced
½ green or red bell pepper, seeded and thinly sliced
4 green onions (including tops), thinly sliced
1 can sliced ripe olives
½ c. red wine

In a large bowl, dissolve 1 tablespoon basil and 1 tablespoon oregano, oat bran and flour in water. Beat for 5 minutes. Add in baking flour until thick. Beat for another 5 minutes. On a floured board, knead the dough until smooth for 5 minutes. Set aside. Set oven to 450.  Place pizza crust on a baking sheet and bake for 10 minutes. Remove from oven and add all toppings. Bake for an additional 10 minutes or until toppings are crisp.

# Pita & Vegetable Pizzas

½ c. chopped onion
1 clove garlic, minced
4 c. seeded and chopped tomatoes
   (about 3 lb whole tomatoes)
1 med yellow bell pepper, finely chopped
3 oz fresh mushrooms, thinly sliced
1 sm zucchini, thinly sliced
3 (6-inch) gluten-free pita bread
2 tsp dried whole oregano
¼ tsp pepper
2 tbsp minced fresh basil leaves
3 tbsp red wine vinegar

Sauté an onion and garlic in 3 tbsp water until tender. Stir in tomatoes, vinegar, basil, oregano and pepper. Bring to a boil, reduce heat, and simmer, uncovered 20 minutes or until sauce is reduced. Set aside. Cut slit around edge of each bread round; carefully split apart. Place split rounds on baking sheet; toast at 450 degrees for 5 minutes or until dry and beginning to brown. Spread ¼-cup tomato sauce mixture evenly over each toasted rounds.  Bake at 450 degrees for about 10 minutes until vegetables are tender. Serves 6.

# Spicy Mushroom Chili

½ c. vinegar
1 tbsp garlic, minced
1 c. water
2 sm whole hot dried red chili peppers
1 tbsp bell pepper, diced
2 tbsp peppercorns (or) cracked
   black pepper
1 lb sm whole mushrooms (fresh
   or canned)

Mix vinegar, bell pepper, peppercorns, garlic and chilies together in a quart jar or small saucepan. Add mushrooms to mix and microwave for 4 minutes at 70% power or heat in small saucepan over medium heat until just below boiling. Strain into a quart jar. Add mushrooms back to strained marinade and cool to room temperature then refrigerate. Marinate at least 4-6 hours before serving. Mushrooms are best the next day, but will keep refrigerated for up to 2 weeks.

8 servings, 4-5 mushrooms each.

## Chili Bean Stuffed Peppers

*4 green peppers*
*2 c. cooked kidney beans*
*3 c. cooked brown rice*
*1 c. corn*
*2 tsp chili powder*
*2 tsp chili salsa*
*1 c. tomato sauce*

Wash peppers and cut off tops. Remove and discard seeds and pulp.

Place in pot with cold water to cover, then bring to a boil; reduce heat and simmer for 5 minutes. Drain, then mix together remaining ingredients. Fill peppers with mixture, place into small baking dish and top with a mixture of salsa and tomato sauce. Cover and bake at 350 degrees for 45 minutes. Uncover, bake another 15 minutes more. Serves 4.

*Note: Corn is a common allergen. We recommend a delayed food allergy test before adding it to this recipe.*

## Chili Ranch Style

*8 oz dry pinto beans*
*2 cloves garlic, minced*
*2 onions, chopped*
*4 oz can green chilies, chopped*
*2 jalapeno peppers, diced*
*28 oz can tomatoes with liquid*
*1 tsp oregano*
*Dash of Tabasco*

Soak beans overnight. Cook about 1 hour until tender. Cook onions and garlic in small amount of water until tender. Add to beans with remaining ingredients and bring to a boil. Simmer 1 hour or until sauce reduces. Serves 4.

# Bell Peppers Stuffed with Mushrooms

*3 lg green peppers*
*1½ c. tomatoes*
*1 c. fresh mushrooms*
*1½ c. cooked lentils, (seasoned*
*  with herbs and drained)*
*1 c. cooked brown rice*
*½ c. diced celery and onion*
*Sprinkle of garlic powder*
*Sprinkle of Mrs. Dash*

Cut peppers in half. Boil for 4 minutes. Sauté 1/3 cup onions and ½ cup celery in a skillet until soft. Mix the onion/celery mixture with all the ingredients. Garnish with black pepper to taste. Bake at 350 for 35 minutes.

# Bell Peppers Stuffed with Mushrooms II

*2 lg bell peppers*
*1 ½ c. tomato sauce*
*2 c. cooked brown rice*
*2 tbsp chopped parsley*
*½ tsp Italian seasoning*

Cut peppers in half lengthwise; remove seeds and membranes. Steam pepper halves until cooked crisp-tender; set aside. Combine ½ cup tomato sauce with cooked brown rice, 1 tablespoon chopped parsley, and ½ teaspoon seasoning.

Heat over moderate heat, stirring gently until well blended. Add a little water if needed to prevent sticking. Spoon remaining tomato sauce into bottom of a 9-inch pie pan. Place pepper halves on top of sauce, then fill with rice mixture. Bake at 350 degrees until hot. Sprinkle with chopped parsley and serve.

Serves 4.

# Stuffed Steamed Peppers in Mustard Sauce

*6 sm green or red peppers with tops cut off and seeds removed*

## Stuffing:

*1½ c. cooked brown rice*
*1 shallot, finely chopped*
*1 tsp finely chopped fresh ginger*
*2 cloves garlic, finely chopped*
*Freshly ground pepper*
*6 tsp vegetable stock*
*1 tsp brown rice flour*
*3½ c. bean sprouts*

## Mustard Sauce:

*1 tsp vinegar*
*2 tsp Dijon mustard*
*3 tsp vegetable stock*

Mix together the brown rice, shallot, ginger, garlic, pepper, vegetable stock and rice flour. Stir fry this mixture for 3 minutes in a wok or frying pan. Add in bean sprouts and cook for another 2 mins. Stuff the peppers with this filling. Steam the peppers for 10 minutes. Mix together the mustard sauce and pour over peppers.

# Bell Peppers Stuffed with Buckwheat

*6 med green or red bell peppers*
*1 c. buckwheat*
*½ c. raisins*
*¼ c. chopped onions*
*Fresh crushed black pepper*
*¾ tsp ground cinnamon*
*2 tbsp chopped fresh mint*
*2 tbsp lemon juice*

Boil buckwheat in 8 cups of water for 30 mins. Drain and set aside. Set oven to 350. Cut off the stem. Chop the pepper remains surrounding the stem. Scoop out ribs and seeds. Saute onions and chopped peppers in 1/3 cup of water in a covered skillet for 10 minutes. Add in lemon juice, cinnamon, mint, raisins, and buckwheat. Stir for 3 minutes then season with pepper. Fill the peppers with the buckwheat mixture. Bake the peppers in a baking pan with 1 inch of water for 45 minutes.

Serves 6.

# Baked Burritos with Spicy Sauce

## Sauce:

1 onion, chopped
2 cloves garlic, pressed
½ c. water
1/3 c. chopped canned green chilies
2 tbsp chili powder
1 tsp cumin
½ tsp ground coriander
½ tsp cayenne
1 (8 oz) can tomato sauce
1 (6 oz) can tomato paste
3½ c. water

## Filling:

1 onion, chopped
1 green pepper, chopped
¾ lb mushrooms, chopped
1/3 c. water
3½ c. chopped zucchini
2 tsp chili powder
1 tsp ground cumin
12-15 medium brown rice tortillas

To make sauce: sauté onion and garlic in ½ cup water for 5 minutes. Add green chilies and spices. Stir and sauté a few more minutes. Add remaining ingredients. Mix well and simmer for 15 minutes; set aside. To make filling: sauté onion, green peppers, and mushrooms in water for 5 minutes. Add zucchini, and spices. Sauté 10 minutes more; set aside. To assemble burritos: spread 1 cup of sauce on bottom of a baking dish. Place 1/3-½ cup filling down the center of each tortilla. Roll up tortillas and place, seam side down, in baking dish. Pour remaining sauce over burritos. Cover and bake at 350 degrees for 30 minutes.

Serves 8 to 10.

# Brown Rice Tortillas

*1 cup brown rice flour*
*1/2 cup water*
*1 tsp Mexican seasoning*

In a bowl, mix the flour and seasoning. Then add water to desired consistency. Dough should be soft, not wet. Add more flour or water to reach the desired consistency. Pinch off small balls of dough and coat them in additional flour. With a rolling pin, flatten out each dough ball until finished. Heat a frying pan. Using no oil, cook each tortilla on both sides until lightly browned. Cool on racks.

Makes 4 tortillas.

# Chili Pie

## *Filling:*

*2 (15 oz) cans kidney beans, drained*
*1 onion, chopped fine*
*1 green bell pepper, chopped fine*
*6 oz tomato paste*
*¼ c. water*
*2 tsp chili powder*
*½ c. red wine vinegar*

Sauté onions and pepper in small amount of water;
add remaining ingredients and heat through

## *Crust:*

*¾ c. unsweetened almond flour*
*¼ c. all-purpose gluten-free baking flour or brown rice flour*
*½ c. water*
*1 egg white or egg substitute*

Let water and eggs sit until they are at room temperature, then mix together. Preheat oven to 375 degrees; combine egg whites and water with dry ingredients. Form a ball with dough and place into pie pan sprayed with non-stick spray. Flatten dough with fingers and form into shape of pie crust. Add filling and bake for 35-40 minutes or until crust is light brown.

Serves 6 to 8.

# Chiles Rellenos

*1 (7 oz) can California green chilies*
*½ inch thick sliced zucchini*
*½ c. all-purpose gluten-free baking flour or brown rice flour*
*8 egg whites or egg substitute*
*1 tbsp raw coconut aminos*
*Sliced green onion tops*

Drain fluid from canned chilies. Remove seeds. Then stuff each chili with one slice of zucchini. Coat the chilies with flour. Beat the egg substance until frothy. Add aminos to an omelete pan. Add in 1/3 cup of "eggs". Lay one stuffed chile in the and spoon eggs over the chile. Cook for 3 mins, turn to other side and cook 3 more minutes. Garnish with green onions & a nice salsa.

Serves 4.

## Enchilada Pie

*1 (16 oz) pkg dried pinto beans*
*1 (16 oz) pkg dried lentils*
*12 brown rice tortillas*
*3 (10 oz) cans enchilada sauce*
*1 (29 oz) can tomato sauce*
*1 (29 oz) can tomato puree*
*4 tbsp onion flakes*
*½ tsp cayenne pepper*
*1 sm can Ortega green chilies (mild)*

Soak pinto beans overnight. Cook several hours until tender. Add lentils the last ¾-hour of cooking. Layer all ingredients in a large baking pan; start with sauce and end with sauce. Bake at 350 degrees for 1½ hours.

## Enchilada Bean Casserole

*4 c. cooked and mashed pinto beans*
*3 c. brown rice*
*1½ c. chopped green onions*
*¾ c. chopped black olives*
*12 brown rice tortillas*
*Use Enchilada Sauce Recipe below*

Spread 2 cups of enchilada sauce on the bottom of a baking dish. Place in one tortilla. On top of tortilla add olives, onions, rice and ½ cup of beans. Repeat this process until all of the ingredients are gone. Bake covered for 30 mins at 350. Serves 8.

## Enchilada Sauce

*½ tsp onion powder*
*½ tsp garlic powder*
*3 tbsp chili powder*
*5 tbsp unsweetened almond flour*
*3 c. tomato sauce*
*3 c. water*

Boil together all of the ingredients in a pan until thick.

# Mexican Pasta Bake

*1 med onion, chopped*
*1 clove garlic, chopped*
*½ tsp cayenne*
*1 tbsp chili powder*
*1 qt undrained canned tomatoes*
*1 tsp oregano*
*½ tsp cumin*
*1 c. gluten-free rice noodle macaroni*
*3 c. cooked black beans*
*1/3 c. sliced olives*
*1 c. (5) broken brown rice tortillas*
*1 c. sliced vegan cheese*

Sauté onion and garlic for 3 minutes to soften. Add cayenne and chili powder and cook briefly. Add tomatoes, oregano, and cumin; bring to a boil. Add pasta and simmer, uncovered for 15 minutes until pasta is just tender. Stir in beans and olives. Preheat oven to 325 degrees. Transfer bean mixture to a shallow 2-quart casserole. Bake for 10 minutes to melt cheese. If casserole is assembled in advance of baking and chilling, increase baking time to approximately 20 minutes or until heated through. Serves 6.

# Green Chili Tamales

*2 c. unsweetened almond flour*
*1¼ c vegetable broth*
*2 c. cooked diced potatoes*
*½ c. pitted olives, chopped*
*½ c. canned green chili salsa*
*1 med onion, chopped*

Mix the vegetable broth and flour together to make a paste. Place 1 ½ tbsp of this dough in a square. Set aside. Mix together salsa, onion, olives and potatoes. Add 1 ½ tbsp of this filling in the middle of each dough square. Place the tamales on a rack in a double boiler. Fill the boiler with 1 inch of water. Steam covered for 45 mins. Serves 6.

# 'Polenta' Pie

## Crust:
1 c. buckwheat groats
½ tsp sage
¼ tsp cumin
½ tsp chili powder
4 c. cold water

## Filling:
1 onion, chopped
1 clove garlic, pressed
½ lb mushrooms, sliced
1 eggplant, diced
2 c. tomato sauce
6 oz tomato paste
1 bay leaf
1/2 tsp basil
1 tsp oregano

Combine buckwheat, sage, cumin, and chili powder in a saucepan. Stir in cold water. Cook while stirring constantly until very thick. Pour into a non-stick oblong baking dish. Bake at 425 degrees for 30 minutes. Remove from oven and let cool for 30 minutes. In the meantime sauté onion, garlic, mushrooms, and eggplant in ½ cup water for 10 minutes. Add remaining ingredients and simmer 20 minutes. Spoon this mixture over the buckwheat crust. Bake at 350 degrees for 30 minutes.

Serves 3 to 4.

# Cauliflower 'Spanish' Mock Rice & Veggies

2 heads cauliflower, separated into flowerettes
2 lg bell peppers, diced
4 lg stalks celery, diced
3 tbsp chili powder, (or to taste)
4 tbsp onion flakes
1 (46 oz) can tomato juice
1 clove minced garlic
Sea salt to taste

Place all ingredients in a large pot. Bring to a boil. Simmer over low heat until cauliflower becomes tender. Mash with a potato masher until the cauliflower breaks into small rice-like pieces. Continue to simmer until mixture is the consistency of Spanish rice.

## Salsa Fresca

**4 med tomatoes, minced**
**½ sm. onion, minced**
**8 sprigs cilantro, minced**
**1/3 c. red wine vinegar**
**2 serrano or jalapeno peppers, diced**
**½ c. water**

Mix all ingredients and serve or chill first and serve. Best when served very fresh but will keep for 2 days in refrigerator. Yield 2 cups.

## Santa Fe Salsa

**1 c. finely chopped tomato**
**½ c. finely chopped purple onion**
**1 (4 oz) can chopped green chilies, drained**
**1 lg clove garlic, minced**
**1/8 tsp Mrs. Dash extra spicy seasoning**

Mix all ingredients and serve.
Yield: about 2 cups.

## Salsa Verde Green

**½ lb fresh tomatillos**
**4-6 cloves garlic**
**1 c. fresh cilantro leaves**
**1 tbsp fresh green chiles or pickled jalapeno pepper**

Remove brown husks from tomatillos. Wash thoroughly and cut into chunks. Place all ingredients in a blender or food processor and chop finely but do not liquefy.

Makes 1 cup.

## Tofu Tacos

*1 onion, diced*
*1 green bell pepper, diced*
*1 tsp paprika*
*Water for sautéing*
*1 lb almond tofu, cut into chunks*
*2 tbsp tomato puree*
*Dash of Tabasco*
*6 brown rice tortillas*

In a large frying pan, sauté onion, bell pepper, and paprika in a small amount of water for 3-5 minutes. Crumble tofu into small pieces and add to pan; sauté for several minutes. Add 2 tablespoons of water and tomato puree. Cook until mixture is heated thoroughly. Remove from heat. Stuff tortillas with mixture. Serves 6.

## Broccoli with Water Chestnuts

2½ c. broccoli, roughly chopped
3 tbsp bean sprouts
2 cloves garlic, finely chopped
2 tsp finely chopped fresh ginger
½ c. water chestnuts, thinly sliced
8 tbsp vegetable stock
2 tbsp bamboo shoots, thinly sliced
1 tbsp raw coconut aminos
1 tsp unsweetened almond flour

Using 3 tbsp of vegetable stock, stir fry ginger, garlic, bean sprouts and broccoli for 4 mins. Add in bamboo shoots and chestnuts and cook for 2 additional mins. Meanwhile whisk together the remaining vegetable stock, flour and aminos. Add the liquid to the pan. Simmer for 3 minutes. Serve.

## Chinese Broccoli, Cauliflower & Almonds

1 tbsp water
2 cloves garlic, minced
4 tbsp dry sherry
½ c. chopped almonds
3 c. broccoli, cut into bite-size pieces
3 c. cauliflower, cut into bite-size pieces

Sauté garlic in a large skillet or wok, using water in place of oil. Add the sherry and water. Turn the heat to moderate and add the broccoli and cauliflower. Stir quickly to coat the veggies with the liquid. Stir fry just until the pieces are well distributed. Top with almonds. Serves 4.

## Red Cooked Cabbage

*1 Chinese cabbage, roughly chopped*
*1 tbsp finely chopped fresh ginger*
*1 clove garlic, finely chopped*
*1 shallot, finely chopped*
*1 red chili, finely chopped*
*1½ c. vegetable stock*
*1 tbsp fresh orange juice*

Stir fry cabbage, ginger, garlic, shallots and chili in half the stock for 3 minutes. Reduce heat. Add remaining stock and orange juice. Simmer for another 5 minutes and serve.

## Chinese Eggplant

*4 med long eggplants*
*4 cloves garlic, crushed*
*1 thumb-size piece ginger root*
*2 stalks green onions*
*3 tbsp water*
*¼ tsp crushed red chili pepper*
*(optional)*

Cut eggplant into ¼ x 1 inch pieces. Cook in a small amount of boiling water until almost done, 5 to 8 minutes. Drain.

Serves 6.

## Sweet and Sour Green Beans

*1 onion, chopped*
*2 carrots, sliced*
*1 clove garlic, minced*
*1 green pepper, chopped*
*2 tomatoes, sliced*
*2½ c. cooked green beans*
*¾ c. canned pineapple chunks*
*1½ tbsp unsweetened almond flour*
*1½ tbsp raw coconut aminos*
*1/3 c. vegetable broth*
*½ c. apple juice*
*½ c. wine vinegar*
*1½ tbsp sherry*

Sauté onion, carrots, and garlic. Add green pepper and cook about 1 minute longer. Add pineapple, tomatoes and green beans and cook for 2 more minutes.

In a bowl, combine flour, aminos, apple juice, vegetable broth, wine vinegar, and sherry. Pour on top of beans and cook until sauce bubbles and thickens.

Serves 6.

## Stir Fry Sauce

*1 clove garlic, minced*
*1½ tbsp raw coconut aminos*
*2½ tbsp unsweetened almond flour*
*½ tsp ginger*

Sauté garlic over low heat. Pour stock over garlic and add aminos, sherry, and ginger. Turn the heat to medium. Dissolve the flour in a little cold water. Add the flour mixture. Let the sauce boil slowly until it has thickened, stirring almost continuously. Pour this over the stir fry veggies once they are done and serve over brown rice.

## Stir-fry

*½ c. vegetable stock*
*½ sm onion, chopped*
*1 clove garlic, minced*
*4 carrots, sliced or grated*
*4 celery stalks, chopped*
*½ head cabbage*
*¼ green pepper, diced*
*4 c. bean sprouts*
*12 lg mushrooms, chopped*
*1 bunch scallions, chopped*
*1 can water chestnuts, sliced*

Heat the stock. Add onion and garlic. Stir fry 1-2 minutes. Add the carrots and celery. Stir them quickly to seal in their juices. When these are about half done, add in cabbage and green pepper. When these veggies are nearly cooked, add in bean sprouts, mushrooms, scallions, and water chestnuts. Stir continuously, until all the veggies are tender crisp.

# Green Peppers and Chinese Mushrooms

*3 lg green peppers, diced*
*8 Chinese mushrooms, soaked in*
*  hot water for 30 minutes, remove*
*  stems, cut into quarters*
*4 tbsp vegetable stock*
*1 tbsp water*
*1 tsp unsweetened almond flour*
*Freshly ground pepper*
*3 cloves garlic, chopped*

Stir fry mushrooms, garlic, and green peppers with stock in non-stick frying pan for 3 minutes. Mix water and almond flour. Add to frying pan and simmer for 2 minutes. Season with pepper. Serve hot.

# Pumpkin Treat

*1 c. water*
*3 c. pumpkin, diced*
*1 clove garlic, chopped*
*1 tbsp fresh ginger, chopped*
*3 tsp toasted sesame seeds*
*1 tsp raw coconut aminos*
*Freshly ground pepper*
*1 tbsp almond flour*
*with 1 tsp cold water*

Bring water to the boil and stir fry pumpkin for 15 minutes with garlic clove and ginger. Add aminos and pepper; simmer for another 2 minutes. Thicken with almond flour mix. Simmer for 1 minute. Sprinkle with sesame seeds and serve.

## Chinese Fruit Salad

1 c. watermelon balls
1 c. honeydew melon balls
2 c. diced fresh pineapple or
   canned unsweetened pieces
1 c. kiwi fruit circles
2 c. fresh lychees
1 c. sliced fresh mango
1 tbsp finely chopped fresh ginger
¼ clove crushed garlic
1 c. fresh orange juice
1 c. unsweetened pineapple juice
1 c. diced apple

Combine all ingredients. Chill
before serving.

## Raw Chinese Salad

4 c. shredded Chinese cabbage
2 c. diced water chestnuts
1 sm white onion, finely chopped
2 shallots, sliced
2 c. carrots, grated
2 c. bean sprouts
1 tbsp toasted sesame seeds
1 c. fresh orange juice
1 tbsp raw coconut aminos

Combine all ingredients and serve.

## Chilled Noodle Salad

5 c. brown rice noodles
1 c. carrots, grated
½ c. diced shallots
½ c. finely shredded red cabbage
1 clove garlic, chopped
1 tsp chopped fresh ginger
1 tbsp water
¼ c. fresh lemon juice
2 tsp toasted sesame seeds

Combine all ingredients and serve.

# Chinese Noodles

8 dried Chinese mushrooms, soaked
  for 30 minutes in hot water, discard
  stems and finely slice
¼ c. bean curd, diced
2 c. bean sprouts
1 c. sliced shallots
2 fresh red chilies, chopped
2½ c. fresh rice noodles, cut into
  thin strips
1 green pepper, finely sliced
1 red pepper, finely sliced
5 tsp vegetable stock

## Sauce:

1 tsp unsweetened almond flour
2 cloves garlic, chopped
2 tsp chopped fresh ginger
2 tsp sesame seeds
Freshly ground pepper
1 tsp water
1 tbsp mild to medium
  hot curry powder
3 tbsp vegetable stock
1 tbsp fresh orange juice
1 tbsp dry sherry

Bring a large pan of water to a boil. Meanwhile mix sauce ingredients together in a large bowl. Cook the noodles in the boiling water for 30 seconds
to one minute then drain. In 2 tbsp of vegetable stock sauté the bean curd
for 1 minute in a wok or pan.  Remove and set aside. In 3 tbsp of vegetable
stock sauté the chilies, peppers, mushrooms, shallots and bean sprouts for 2
mins.  Mix together vegetables, bean curd, noodles and sauce in the pan and
continue to heat for 3 mins. Remove from heat and serve.

## Rice Noodles and Green Peppers in Black Bean Sauce

*1 tsp black beans soaked in cold water*
  *for 15 minutes to remove excess salt,*
    *drain and mash*
*3 c. fresh rice noodles, cut into strips*
*1 tbsp finely chopped fresh ginger*
*2 shallots, finely chopped*
*2 tbsp dry sherry*
*2 med green peppers, seeded and cut strips*
*3 tbsp vegetable stock*
*2 tsp unsweetened almond flour*
*3 cloves garlic, finely chopped*

Stir fry garlic, black beans, shallots, ginger, and green peppers in a non-stick frying pan with tablespoons of stock for 3 minutes. Bring a large saucepan of water to the boil. Plunge rice noodles in for 1 minute. Remove and drain. Mix 2 tablespoons vegetable stock, almond flour, and sherry. Add to frying pan. Add rice noodles and stir over low heat for 2 minutes. Serve hot.

## Rice Noodles w/ Lettuce and Mushrooms

*1 sm lettuce, roughly chopped*
*6 dried mushrooms, soaked in hot water*
  *for 30 minutes, discard stems,*
    *and cut into quarters*
*2 tsp unsweetened almond flour*
*3 cloves garlic, finely chopped*
*1 tbsp finely chopped fresh ginger*
*3 c. fresh rice noodles, cut into strips*
*Freshly ground pepper*
*1 shallot, finely chopped*
*1 c. basic vegetables*
*2 tbsp dry sherry*

Stir fry lettuce, mushrooms, garlic, ginger, and shallots with half the stock in a non-stick frying pan for 3 minutes. Bring a large saucepan of water to boil. Plunge in noodles for 1 minute. Remove and drain. Mix almond flour and sherry with remaining stock and add to frying pan. Stir in rice noodles. Season with pepper and simmer for 2 minutes.
Serve hot.

# Spicy Noodles

*6 tbsp rice vinegar*
*2 tbsp finely chopped scallions*
*6 tsp coconut aminos*
*1 tsp chili powder*
*½ lb brown rice noodles*
*2 tbsp finely chopped roasted cashews*
*1 tsp minced garlic*

 In a bowl mix together the aminos, chili powder, scallions, garlic and vinegar.  Meanwhile bring 8 cups of water to a boil. Add in the noodles. Once the noodles are boiling, add in 1 cup of water.  Cook them until they come to a boil again then drain.  Mix together the sauce and noodles garnishing with cashews on top.

Serves 4.

# Oriental Rice

*2 tsp minced ginger*
*2 lg cloves garlic, minced*
*½ c. vegetable stock*
*3 c. sliced mushrooms*
*2 c. sliced bok choy*
*1 c. diced bell pepper*
*1 c. diced carrots*
*1¼ c. sliced water chestnuts*
*4 c. cooked brown rice*
*1 c. chopped green onions*
*1½ tsp sesame seeds, toasted*

Sauté ginger and garlic in ¼ cup vegetable stock. Add mushrooms, bok choy, bell pepper, carrots, water chestnuts, and rice. Cook until vegetables are tender, adding more vegetable stock as needed. Add green onion and sesame seeds. Makes 10 servings (each 1-cup serving).

# Raw Chop Suey

*2 lg heads Napa cabbage*
*2 med heads bok choy*
*2 c. broccoli flowerettes*
*1/4 c. chopped watercress*
*¼ c. minced parsley*
*4 tbsp lime juice*

*3 c. red bell pepper strips*
*cherry tomatoes for garnish*
*3 sheets nori, crumbled*
*1½ c. mung bean sprouts*
*4 stalks celery, chopped*
*1 c. sliced mushrooms*

Shred the bok choy and napa cabbage in a blender. Place the greens in a bowl with the watercress, parsley and broccoli. Puree the nori and lime juice in a blender and add to the greens mixtures. Stir in the rest of the ingredients and mix well.

Serves 4.

# Chow Mein

*4 c. brown rice noodles*
*4 tbsp vegetable stock*
*1 c. bean sprouts*
*5 dried mushrooms soaked*
  *in hot water for 30 minutes,*
  *discard stems and slice*
*1 c. bamboo shoots*
*3 cloves garlic, chopped*
*1 c. sliced carrots*
*1 c. broccoli flowerettes*
*10 snow peas, trimmed*

## Sauce:

*2 tsp unsweetened almond flour*
*½ c. vegetable stock*
*1 tbsp diced shallots*
*1 tsp chopped fresh ginger*
*Freshly ground pepper*
*2 tbsp dry sherry*

Drop noodles into boiling water. Reduce heat. Simmer for 1 minute and drain. Stir fry remaining ingredients in a non-stick frying pan or wok for 3 minutes with 4 tablespoons of stock. Return drained noodles to frying pan. Mix sauce ingredients. Pour sauce over chow mein and toss for 3 minutes over low heat. Serve hot.

## Oriental Noodles

*1 pkg brown rice ramen*
*1 lb broccoli*
*1 clove garlic, minced*
*1 onion, chopped*
*¾ c. vegetable broth*
*2 carrots, sliced*
*1 red or green bell pepper, sliced*
*¼ lb mushrooms, sliced*
*1 lb almond tofu, cut into cubes*
*2 stalks celery, chopped*

Cut off broccoli flowerettes; peel off and discard tough outside layer of stalks, then cut stalks into ¼-inch thick slices. Slice large broccoli flowerettes in half or third lengthwise. Cook noodles, according to package directions; drain well.

Place other ingredients in wok. Stir fry on high heat for 5-6 minutes until veggies are crisp-tender. Serve over noodles. 4 servings.

## Oriental Stir-Fry with Brown Rice

*Parsley Patch Oriental Blend (no salt, no MSG, no sugar)*
*1 (16 oz) pkg frozen vegetables*
*1 (14 oz) pkg fresh chop suey mix*
*1 (6 oz) pkg frozen Chinese pea pods*

In a non-stick pan; stir fry the above ingredients in a large skillet over medium heat until lightly brown. Add about 1 cup cooked brown rice; stir and blend well. Sprinkle with Oriental Blend seasoning to taste.

## Nick's Spicy Brown Rice and Noodles

*2 c. brown rice*
*¼ c. lentils*
*½ c. brown rice noodles*
*1 clove garlic, minced*
*Onion powder*
*6 c. vegetable broth*
*½ c. chili salsa*

Mix all ingredients, except chili salsa and cook in a large, covered pan for 40 minutes. Add the chili salsa; cover pan again and let sit for 20 minutes without heat. Ready to eat.

## Vegetable Burgers

*2 c. shredded carrot*
*1 c. cooked brown rice*
*½ c. chopped onion*
*½ c. chopped almonds*
*½ c. gluten free bread crumbs*
*1 tbsp parsley, chopped*
*½ tsp ground ginger*
*¼ tsp pepper*
*½ tsp ground coriander*
*1 c. egg whites substitute*
*2 tbsp water*

In a large bowl, stir together carrot, rice, onion, almonds, bread crumbs, parsley, ginger, coriander, and ¼ teaspoon pepper. Stir together egg substitute and water; add to rice mixture and mix well. Cover and chill. Shape rice mixture into 6 patties. Place patties on baking sheet. Broil 3 or 4 inches from heat for 3-5 minutes on each side. 6 servings.

## Vegetable Loaf

*1 c. chopped onion*
*1 c. minced celery*
*1 c. grated raw carrots*
*1 c. finely ground English walnuts*
*1 tsp poultry seasoning*
*1 c. dry toasted gluten-free bread crumbs*
*4 egg whites or egg substitute*
*1 c. vegetable broth*
*1 c. tomato sauce*

Brown onion until tender. Add vegetables, nuts, crumbs, seasonings. Sauté. Mix eggs and vegetable broth. Combine both mixtures; turn into loaf pan, sprayed with non-stick spray. Bake at 350 degrees for 40 minutes. Serve with tomato sauce. Serves 4.

## Garbanzo Meatloaf

*1 pkg gluten free falafel*
*2 egg whites or egg substitute*
*½ c. gluten free oat bran*
*½ sm onion, chopped fine*
*1 clove garlic, minced*
*½ tsp pepper*
*½ tsp sage*
*½ tsp marjoram*
*2 tbsp sugar free ketchup*
*2 tbsp Worcestershire sauce*
*½ tps Dijon mustard*

Combine all ingredients; mix well in a large bowl. Form loaf and place in non-stick loaf pan and bake at 350 degrees for 1 hour or until done. Serves 4.

# Nori Maki Sushi

## Ingredients:
4 sheets dried seaweed
1 c. short-grain brown rice
2 tsp coconut mectar
½ tsp sea salt
2-4 tbsp rice vinegar
2 c. water

## Condiments:
Spicy mustard
Pickled ginger

## Filling ingredients:
Avocado
Carrot, grated
Jicama, grated
Watercress, chopped
Spinach, chopped & cooked
Strips of scallion, bell pepper, or celery
Egg whites or egg substitute, cooked
Toasted sesame seeds
Asparagus, steamed
Green beans
Mushrooms

Cook rice according to instructions. Meanwhile sauté mushrooms and cut into strips. Mix and match the filling ingredients to your desire. In a small saucepan, liquefy coconut nectar salt and vinegar. Pour the mixture over the rice once complete. Using a bamboo mat, place a sheet of seaweed on top and then the seasoned rice. Add in your desired ingredients. Roll the bamboo mat away from you pressing the sushi wrap together. Moisten the outside flap and seal the edges. Slice each into small pieces.
Serves 6.

# Grilled Portobello & Peach Burgers with Sweet Potato Fries

6 portobello mushrooms
6 peaches
6 sweet potatoes
5 spring onions, sliced
6 burger buns of your choice
(gluten-free or use lettuce wraps)
5 roman tomatoes, sliced
Fresh thyme
1 bunch fresh pea sprouts
Vegetable broth
Salt and pepper
1 tbsp salsa

## Marinade:

4 tbsp lemon juice
2 fresh rosemary sprigs
1 tbsp fresh thyme
2 garlic cloves
½ lemon
Salt and pepper

## Guacamole:

4 avocados
5 Roma tomatoes
1 garlic clove
¼ c. cilantro
½ lime
jalapeno pepper

Clean the mushrooms. Pit and halve the peaches. Set aside. Set the oven to 350. Cut the sweet potatoes to 5 inch thick slices. On a baking sheet, drizzle the potatoes with thyme, salt and vegetable broth. Bake for 30 mins. In a small bowl mix together salt, pepper, garlic, thyme and rosemary. Brush the peaches and mushrooms with this mixture. Get the grill to a medium heat and then grill the peaches and mushrooms for 4 minutes on each side brushing the marinade over again. Set aside. Mash the avocados tomatoes, cilantro, garlic and jalapeño in a small bowl. Squeeze over some lime juice for taste and to prevent browning. Put together the burgers and enjoy!

Serves 6.

# Barbecued Lentil Burgers

*1 c. lentils*
*3 c. water*
*1 onion, chopped fine*
*1 clove garlic, crushed*
*2 stalks celery, finely chopped*
*1 carrot, grated*
*½ c. brown rice*
*3 tbsp tomato sauce*
*2 tsp chili powder*

Place lentils and water in a medium saucepan and bring to a boil. Add onion, garlic, celery, and carrot. Reduce heat, cover, and simmer for 30 minutes. Add remaining ingredients. Cook an additional 15 minutes. Remove from heat and let cool. Shape into patties and cook on a non-stick griddle until browned (about 15 minutes).  Serve on gluten-free buns or lettuce wraps with a variety of condiments. Makes 10.

# Oriental Garbanzo Burgers

*1 lb Falafel*
*1/4 c. gluten free oat bran*
*1/2 tsp ginger*
*½ tsp coriander*
*1 tbsp water*

Mix all ingredients together in large bowl. Form into 4 patties and cook in non-stick skillet (use non-stick spray) until browned. Serves 4.

# Lentil Sprout Sloppy Joes

*3 c. lentil sprouts (½ c. dry lentils,*
*  sprouted for 3 days)*
*1 c. organic spaghetti sauce (no-oil)*
*½ c. sliced onions*
*10 gluten-free hamburger buns*

In processor, grind lentil sprouts with spaghetti sauce (no-oil, meatless, sugarless) to make a thick mixture. Heat and serve over warmed, gluten-free hamburger buns or lettuce wraps. May top with chopped onion, if desired.

# Bean & Vegetable Loaf

*8 oz dried white northern beans*
*4 c. water*
*3 cloves garlic, minced*
*1 bouquet garnish: (4 sprigs parsley, 1 tsp thyme,*
*  1 bay leaf, ½ tsp crushed red pepper)*
*5 lg Swiss chard leaves, stems removed*
*¼ lb fresh whole string beans*
*¼ lb fresh whole okra*
*¼ lb fresh small whole carrots*
*5 artichoke hearts*
*½ c. egg whites or egg substitute, slightly beaten*

Cook beans in water with bouquet garnish for 1½ hours. Drain and puree beans in blender. Mix pureed beans with slightly beaten eggs and garlic. Blanch Swiss chard leaves, string beans, and okra for 3 minutes in boiling water and refresh in cold water. Line a non-stick 6-cup loaf pan with overlapping Swiss chard leaves. Spread a ¼ layer of bean puree, then a layer of vegetables. Continue alternating bean paste and vegetables. The first layer should be okra, then artichokes, then carrots, then string beans, end with beaten paste. Cover with foil and place in a baking pan with 1-inch hot water.

Bake in a preheated oven at 350 degrees for 30-45 minutes or until mixture is firm. Serve hot with a tomato sauce or cold with vinaigrette dressing (no- oil). Serves 8 to 10.

# Red Bean Burgers

*4 c. cooked red or pink beans, drained*
*4 green onions, sliced thin*
*½ c. red bell pepper, chopped*
*½ c. chopped fresh parsley*
*¼ tsp cayenne*
*Tabasco to taste*
*½ tsp thyme*
*½ c. Slim Blend*
*¼ tsp garlic powder*

Process the garlic powder, thyme, Tabasco, cayenne, parsley, ¼ Slim Blend, red pepper, onions and beans in a blender until smooth. Using the remaining Slim Blend to mold together the beans patties. Cook in a skillet for 5 minutes on each side. Serve in a gluten free bun or lettuce wrap topped with your favourite condiments.

# Sweet Potato Veggie Burger

*2 cans cannellini white beans, drained*
*1 lg sweet potato, baked & mashed*
*2 tbsp tahini*
*1 tsp lemon pepper seasoning OR Cajun seasoning*
*¼ c. gluten-free flour*
*Salt to taste if needed*
*2 tsp coconut nectar*
*Gluten-free bread crumbs*
*1 tbsp vegetable broth*

## Burgers:
*Avocado*
*Dijon mustard*
*Gluten free buns or lettuce wraps*
*Romaine lettuce*
*Onion*
*Olive oil*

Mix together the sweet potato and white beans with the seasoning and flour. Roll together patties. Meanwhile heat 1 tbsp vegetable broth in a saucepan. Coat patties in bread crumbs. Then brown in the saucepan on both side. Serve in a bun with your favourite condiments.

Serves 8.

# Artichoke & Pinto Bean Casserole

*2 (1 lb) pinto beans*
*1 (1 lb) artichoke hearts, drained and chopped*
*1/8 tsp each cayenne and ground cloves*
*½ tsp ground cumin*

Preheat oven to 350 degrees. Empty 1 can of beans and liquid into a 9-inch square baking pan. Drain and rinse the other can of beans, then roughly chop the beans. Add chopped beans and artichokes to the whole beans. Add spices and chili sauce; mix together well. Set pan in oven, uncovered, and bake for 30 minutes.

# Zucchini Casserole

*4 low-sodium bouillon cubes, melted*
*Juice of ½ lemon*
*2 onions, thinly sliced*
*1 tsp red pepper, crushed*
*6 sm zucchini, cut in ½-inch slices*
*2 cloves garlic, crushed*
*4 ripe tomatoes cut in ¼-inch slices*

In a covered casserole, add in the zucchini, tomatoes, onions, garlic and red pepper. Drizzle with lemon juice. Add in bouillon cubes. Bake for 45 mins at 325.

# Creole Casserole

*1 med size eggplant, peeled and thickly sliced*
*2 ½ c tomato puree*
*2 c water*
*1 ½ c thinly sliced mushrooms*
*1 ½ c coarsely chopped onions*
*1 c green chili salsa*
*1 t Italian seasoning*
*½ t garlic powder*
*3 c fresh or frozen okra, cut into lg pieces*
*1/3 c gluten-free flour*

Soak eggplant in cold water to cover for 30 minutes. Meanwhile, combine tomato puree, water, mushrooms, onions, salsa, Italian seasoning, and garlic powder in a large saucepan; bring to a boil. Reduce heat and simmer, uncovered for 20 minutes. Add okra and cook for another 5 minutes; set aside.

Preheat oven to 350 degrees. Pat eggplant slices dry with paper towels. Dredge eggplant slices in flour. Place them on a baking sheet and bake for 10 minutes or until browned. Increase oven temperature to 375 degrees. Line a 9 x 11 inch baking dish with eggplant slices and pour okra mixture over them. Bake for 30 minutes. Makes 8 servings.

# Fruit Rice Stuffing

1½ c. chopped onion
1½ c.chopped celery
½ c. chopped parsley
7 c. cooked brown rice
1 tsp marjoram
½ c. chopped nuts
½ tsp thyme
½ tsp sage
Salt and pepper
3 egg whites or egg substitute,
  lightly beaten
¾ c. vegetable broth
6 oz mixed dried fruit
½ c. raisins

Sauté onions, celery, and parsley. Remove from heat and combine with rice in large bowl. Stir in marjoram, thyme, and sage. Season to taste with salt and pepper. Add eggs, stock, fruit and nuts. Mix well.

# Almond Rice Pilaf

¼ c. minced onion
½ c. chopped blanched almonds
1 c. raw brown rice
Pepper to taste
2 c. hot vegetable broth

Sauté onion until it is transparent. Do not let it brown. Add almonds and sauté for 1-2 minutes or until barely golden. Add rice and sauté until rice is transparent, stirring constantly. Add hot broth all at once, mixture will sizzle. Cover tightly. Simmer on low heat for 30-40 minutes or until rice is ten-der. Season with pepper.

Makes 4 servings.

# Saffron Rice

½ tsp crushed saffron threads
3 tbsp water
1/3 c. currants or raisins
¼ c. shelled, chopped pistachios or pine nuts
3 c. vegetable broth or water
1 tbsp Veg-It
Lg pinch of cinnamon
1½ c. long-grain brown or basmati rice

Dissolve the saffron in water. Sauté the currants or raisins, nuts and rice. Stir over low heat for several minutes, then add the stock or water and dissolved saffron. Stir once, raise the heat, and bring to a boil, then lower heat, cover and simmer for 35 minutes or until steamed.

Serves 6 to 8.

# Indian Spice Rice

*2 c. cooked brown rice*
*1 c. chopped onion*
*1½ c. chopped celery*
*1 c. frozen green peas, thawed and rinsed*
*   to separate*
*2 tbsp chopped mint leaves*
*1 tbsp onion powder*
*1 tsp curry powder*
*½ c. orange juice*

Sauté onion and celery in non-stick pan (use non-stick spray) for about 3-5 minutes on low heat. Add orange juice and continue cooking until liquid is almost evaporated. Stir in mint leaves, onion and curry powder, and blend to combine flavors. Stir in the rice and peas and heat through. Serves 4 to 5.

## Squash Casserole

*6-8 med yellow squash, sliced*
*1 lg onion, chopped*
*3 stalks celery, diced*
*½ green bell pepper, diced*
*2 tbsp water*
*1 (13 oz) almond milk*
*½ c. gluten-free toasted bread*
*crumbs*
*¼ tsp white pepper*
*Sea salt as needed*

Preheat oven to 350 degrees. Boil squash until tender, not mushy, and mash. Sauté onion, celery, and green pepper in 2 tablespoons water in a non-stick pan. Add to squash along with milk, bread crumbs and white pepper, mix well. Pour into a non-stick pan and sprinkle top with more bread crumbs.

Bake at 350 degrees for about 45 minutes. Serves 6 to 8.

## Succotash

*5 c. peeled, diced potatoes*
*3 c. low-sodium vegetable stock*
*1 c. coarsely chopped onions*
*2½ c. baby lima beans*
*2 c. diced fresh tomatoes*
*1 lg clove garlic, minced*
*1 tbsp water*
*½ tsp dried thyme*
*½ tsp poultry seasoning*

Place potatoes, stock and onions in a large pot. Bring to a boil and cook until potatoes are barely tender and almost all of the stock has been absorbed. If potatoes are cooked before all stock is absorbed, puree 1/3 of the vegetables and stock in a food processor or blender and return it to the pot; this will thicken the mixture.

Stir in lima beans, tomatoes, garlic, water, thyme, and poultry seasoning, and cook for another 10 minutes or until frozen vegetables are heated through and flavors are well blended.

Makes 10 servings.

# Tortilla Azteca Soup

*Baked brown rice tortilla pieces*
*1 tbsp water*
*2/3 c. pine nuts*
*¾ c. walnut halves*
*1 lg red onion, chopped*
*2 cloves garlic, minced*
*12 c. vegetable broth*
*4 c. diced, peeled butternut or acorn squash*
*¾ c. toasted, shelled pumpkin seeds*
*1 lg avocado*

Set oven to 400 and bake tortillas for 10 minutes. In a pan sauté pine nuts and walnuts until browned in 1 tbsp of water. Remove nuts and set aside. Sauté garlic and onion in 2 tbsp vegetable broth until golden. In a large pot add the squash, vegetable broth, garlic and onion and bring to a boil. Simmer covered until tender. Cook for 6 more mins. Garnish with pumpkin seeds, tortilla strips, nuts and diced avocado.

# Chilled Tomato Herb Soup

*2 vegetable bouillon cubes*
*1 c. boiling water*
*3 c. tomato juice*
*1 sm onion, grated*
*1 c. celery, chopped*
*1 green pepper, minced*
*1 clove garlic*
*3 tbsp lemon juice*
*Dash of Tabasco sauce*
*2 tbsp dried basil*
*1 cucumber diced*
*2 ripe tomatoes, peeled and diced*

Dissolve the cubes in water. Cool slightly, and then add the next 4 ingredients. Cut the garlic in half and stick a toothpick through both halves. Add to the mixture. Mix and refrigerate for several hours. Just before serving, remove the garlic and add remaining ingredients.

Serve cold. Serves 6.

## Stuffed Acorn Squash

*1 sm acorn squash, trimmed and halved*
*1 tart apple, sliced*
*1 tbsp chopped pecans*
*1 tbsp raisins, halved*
*½ tsp cinnamon*
*1/3 c. apple juice*

Set oven to 375. Place squash soft side down in a baking pan with ½ in water. Cover and bake for 35 mins. Sauté nuts, raisins, apple juice and apple slices in a pan until soft. Juice should thicken in 4 mins. Add cinnamon. Remove fiber and seeds from squash. Add the squash flesh to the apple mixture. Scoop back into shells. Bake in oven 5 mins.

Serves 2.

## Azuki Beans and Squash

*1 c. azuki beans*
*1 strip seaweed*
*Spring water*
*1 c. buttercup squash, cubed but not peeled*
*Sea salt to taste*

Soak the beans overnight. In the bottom of a pot put the seaweed and then the squash. Top the final layer off with beans. Add enough water to cover the squash layer. Bring to a boil slowly over low heat. Cover for 15 mins. Cook for an hour until the beans are almost done. Add in sea salt and cold water. Cook for another 30 minutes until water has evaporated.

Serves 2.

# Buckwheat Stew

*1/3 c. each: pinto beans, red beans, lentils,*
*  split peas, and black eyed peas*
*½ c. buckwheat*
*6 c. fresh water*
*24 oz low-sodium vegetable juice*
*Sea salt*
*1 chopped onion*
*Any favorite vegetables*
*Garlic powder*

Soak beans overnight, covering with 2-inches of water. Drain off and rinse the next morning. Simmer in a large pot soaked beans, water, juice, garlic powder, and Sea Salt. Simmer, covered over a very low heat for 6 hours, and then add onion and buckwheat. Simmer 45 minutes, and then add any vegetables. Simmer 30 more minutes.

Serves 10.

# Summer Stew

*2 onions, sliced*
*2 cloves garlic, crushed*
*6 sm zucchini, sliced ½-inch thick*
*4 sm yellow crookneck squash, sliced ½-inch thick*
*1 green pepper, coarsely chopped*
*2 c. snow peas, trimmed and left whole*
*3 c. tomato chunks*
*1 tsp basil*
*1½ tsp dill weed*
*1½ tsp paprika*

In a large saucepan, sauté garlic and onions in ½ cup water until soft. Add in ½ cup water, tomatoes, peas, pepper and squash. Cover and simmer for 20 mins. Add in seasoning and cook for 10 more mins.

Serves 8.

# Gazpacho

2 lg cucumbers, peeled
4-5 ripe big boy-type tomatoes,
   peeled if you have the time (to peel,
   pierce skin and place in pan of boiling
   water 1 minute or microwave until the
   skin easily slips off)
1/3-½ c. chopped green scallions
2 cloves garlic
1/3 c. red wine vinegar or herbed vinegar,
   such as tarragon, oregano or raspberry
1 c. vegetable stock (low sodium)
1 c. low-sodium vegetable juice
Few drops of Tabasco, to your taste
3 tbsp fresh basil or 1 tbsp dried
Minced lemon wedges
Gluten-free bread, rubbed with garlic,
   toasted until dry and cut into
   cubes for croutons
1 bell pepper, cut with seeds and pits
   discarded

Place all ingredients in a food processor, process with an on-off motion, until chunky and partially pureed. Refrigerate 1 hour before serving. Add lemon, if desired.

Serves 8 to 10.

# Ratatouille Especial

2 c. eggplant, diced
1 c. zucchini, diced
½ c. green bell pepper, chopped
1½ c. cooked mushrooms, chopped
½ c. onions, cut in chunks
4 c. cooked brown rice
2 c. water
2 tbsp vegetable broth seasoning

In large pot combine water and remaining ingredients, except rice, and cook over medium heat for 30 minutes. Serve over hot cooked brown rice.

Serves 4 to 6.

# Cauliflower Curry

1 head cauliflower, cut into 1-inch pieces
2 onions, chopped fine
½ c. lentils
½ tsp chili powder
1 tsp curry powder
Juice of 1 lemon

Sauté onion in small amount of water 5 minutes. Add cauliflower, lentils, and spices. Add cup of water and cook until cauliflower is tender on low flame. Add lemon juice.

Serves 4.

# Healthy Stew

1 c. garbanzo beans, dry
1 c. kidney beans, dry
1 onion, sliced
1 clove garlic, crushed
1 tsp curry powder
3 carrots sliced
2 zucchini, sliced
2 c. gluten-free pasta, cooked
½ c. quinoa
2 c. fresh spinach, chopped
1 tbsp lemon juice

Place beans in a large pot with 2-quarts water. Soak overnight or bring to a boil; cook for 2 minutes. Turn off heat and let rest for 1-hour. Then add onion, garlic and curry powder. Bring to a boil, reduce heat, and cook for 2-hours. When beans are almost tender, add carrots and zucchini. Cook for 30 minutes more, then add pasta and quinoa. Cook an additional 5 minutes. Serve immediately.

Serves 6.

# Armenian Stew

¼ c. dried garbanzo beans
1½ c. dried apricots
5 c. vegetable broth
1 c. lentils
3 red onions, sliced
2 tbsp coconut nectar

Soak the garbanzo beans overnight. Soak the dried apricots for 1-hour. In a large pan, bring the soaked apricots and their water to a boil. Add the soaked, drained garbanzo beans and 1-cup vegetable broth. Bring to a boil; cook for 30 minutes. Add the lentils, onion and 4-cups vegetable broth to the pot. Bring to a boil. Lower heat, cover, cook about 2 hours until garbanzos are tender. Add coconut nectar and mix well. Serve over brown rice.

Serves 8.

# Raw BBQ Stew

½ lg red bell pepper, diced
½ lg green bell pepper, diced
¼ c. chopped parsley
1 c. broccoli flowerettes
3 stalks celery, trimmed and chopped
1 c. sliced mushrooms
1 c. cubed zucchini

## Sauce:

¼ med onion, chopped
6 med tomatoes, shopped
1 sm clove garlic, pressed
1/3 c. minced cilantro
¼ tsp chili powder
1 c. mixed salad greens

In a large bowl, combine vegetable ingredients. Set aside. Puree sauce ingredients in a food processor. Add puree to vegetable mixture and stir to combine. Arrange salad greens on 4 plates. Top with stew and garnish with banana squash.

Serves 4.

# French Vegetable Soup

8 c. water
2 onions, coarsely chopped
2 potatoes, chopped coarsely
1 clove garlic, crushed
2 stalks celery, thickly sliced
1 carrot, thickly sliced
½ lb mushrooms, sliced
4 zucchini, thickly sliced and cut in half
2 leeks, sliced or bunch of green onions sliced
1 c. fresh or frozen peas
1 c. chopped cauliflower pieces
1 tsp thyme
1 tsp dill weed
1 tsp marjoram
1 tsp. basil
Fresh-ground black pepper
2 c. chopped broccoli pieces
1 c. dry white wine

In a large pot, add carrots, celery, garlic, potatoes, onions and 8 cups of water. Bring to a boil. Simmer for 15 minutes. Add in the rest of the ingredients and cook 30 more mins. Garnish with green onions.

Serves 10.

## Beet Walnut Soup

*4 lg beets, cooked and chopped (about 4 c.)*
*2 tbsp vegetable broth*
*1 Granny Smith apple, peeled and chopped*
*1 med onion, chopped*
*5 stalks of celery, chopped*
*3 cloves of garlic, chopped*
*1/3 c. raw walnuts*
*64 oz vegetable broth + more if needed*
*1 tsp sea salt*
*Optional toppings: dill, chives*

Heat a large soup pot to medium-high heat and pour in the 2 tablespoons of vegetable broth. Put the onion in the pan and sauté for about 5 minutes, or until the onions become translucent. Add the apple, celery, garlic, and walnuts and stir frequently for 5 minutes longer. Add the chopped beets and 2-cups of broth to the onion mixture. Using a blender or food processor, liquefy all. Return beet mixture to the pot, stir in the remaining broth, and bring the soup to a boil over medium-high heat. Reduce heat to low and simmer for 15 minutes. Add salt to taste. Serve immediately or chilled. Top with dill and chives. Serve hot or chilled.

## Beet Borscht

*3 c. water*
*½ c. salt-free tomato juice*
*1 med onion, finely chopped*
*¼ head cabbage, finely shredded*
  *(about 1½ c.)*
*2 tbsp fresh lemon juice*
*1 sm beet, cooked, peeled, and*
  *julienned*
*1 tbsp cider vinegar*
*2 tbsp apple juice*

In a large saucepan, combine 3-cups water, tomato juice, onion and cabbage. Bring to a boil, reduce heat, and simmer (covered) about 15 minutes until vegetables are tender. Add remaining ingredients and mix thoroughly. Makes 4 servings. This soup freezes well.

## Black Bean Soup with Chilled Spiced Rice

*3 beef bouillon cubes*
*5 c. minced dried onion*
*1 med green pepper, seeded and chopped (¾ c.)*
*3 cloves garlic, minced or pressed*
*1½ tsp ground cumin*
*1½ tsp dried oregano*
*2 (15 oz) cans black beans drained (pinto or*
  *red beans can be substituted)*
*1 (4 oz) can chopped green chilies*
*2 tbsp cider vinegar*
*Chilled spiced rice*

In 3-quart saucepan, combine all ingredients. Stir, bring to boil, cover, simmer 20-30 minutes. Ladle into bowls, top with a generous spoonful of Chilled Spiced Rice.

### *Chilled Spiced Rice:*

The rice is best when made the night before or at least 30 minutes before serving to allow flavors to blend.

Combine ½ cup finely chopped green onion, ½ teaspoon oregano, ¼ cup each no-oil Italian salad dressing and cider vinegar. Mix with 3 cups cooked brown rice. Chill thoroughly before serving. This distinctive contrast of temperatures and textures make this an especially enjoyable main dish. Serve it with a green salad topped with canned mandarin orange sections and creamy avocado slices with poppy seed dressing. Pass crusty, gluten-free rolls to complete the meal.

## Broccoli Lemon Soup

*1 c. broccoli, chopped*
*2 c. vegetable broth*
*2 egg whites or egg substitute*
*¼ c. lemon juice*
*¼ c. cooked brown rice or rice pasta*
*1 tbsp sweet basil*
*1 clove garlic*
*1 carrot, diced*
*¼ c. diced onion*
*1 tbsp apple juice*

In heavy bottomed saucepan, add all ingredients, except lemon and eggs. Simmer ½ hour. Beat eggs together with lemon juice. Add to soup. Makes 4-6 servings.

## Lima Leek Soup

*1 leek, white part only, finely chopped*
*2 c. cooked dried lima beans*
*1 c. chopped watercress*
*2 c. vegetable broth*
*2 tbsp lemon juice (to taste)*

Sauté leek in vegetable broth or a little water. Add balance of vegetable broth and lima beans. Cover and simmer ½-hour. Let the mixture cool to room temperature. Puree in a blender or food processor. Mix in lemon juice and pepper to taste.

## Chilled Avocado Bean Soup

*2 (10½ oz) cans vegetable broth (chilled)*
*½ c. kidney beans*
*½ c. green beans*
*Dill weed*
*Dash of lemon juice*
*2 ripe avocados, diced*
*1 oz sherry*

Put chilled broth in blender; add diced avocados, sherry, and lemon juice. Blend well. Sprinkle with dill weed.

## Mineralizing Miso Soup

*5 brazil nuts*
*2 tsp dried sea veggies, ground into a powder (kelp, dulse, sea lettuce, etc.)*
*1 tbsp coconut water*
*2 cloves garlic*
*4 tbsp chickpea miso paste*
*½ tsp cayenne pepper*
*½ c. carrots, roughly chopped*
*4 c. warm water*

Place all ingredients into a high-powered blender. Blend on high for 45 seconds to 1 minute.

## Curried Cream of Broccoli Soup

*1 lg onion, chopped (1 c.)*
*2 cloves garlic, chopped (2 tsp)*
*¾ tsp curry powder, or more to taste*
*1 c. almond milk*
*Freshly ground black pepper, if desired, to taste*
*1 c. water*
*1-2/3 c. vegetable broth*
*1 bunch broccoli (about 1 lb) cut into flowerettes, and stems cut into ½-inch slices*
*1 lg potato, peeled and cut into ½-inch cubes*

In a large saucepan, add 2 tablespoons vegetable broth and sauté the onion and garlic for a few minutes. Add the curry, pepper, broth, and water to the pan and bring the soup to a boil. Add the broccoli and potato. When mixture returns to a boil reduce the heat, cover the pan and simmer soup for about 20 minutes or until the vegetables are tender. Puree the soup in batches in a blender or food processor. Return the puree to the pan, stir in the milk, and cook the soup over low heat until it is hot but do not boil it.

# Corn Chowder

*3 c. fresh or frozen corn kernels*
*2 c. low sodium vegetable stock*
*1 celery stalk, finely chopped*
*1 onion, finely chopped*
*1 carrot, peeled and finely chopped*
*1 potato, peeled and diced*
*4 tbsp potato starch*
*1 red bell pepper, seeded and finely chopped*
*4 garlic cloves, finely chopped*
*4 oz canned green chilies, rinsed and chopped*
*¼ tsp white pepper*
*2 tbsp natural rice vinegar*

In a blender, puree 1½ cups corn kernels and 1 cup vegetable stock until smooth. Transfer to a large saucepan and add remaining corn and vegetable stock, celery, onion, carrot, potato, pepper and garlic. Bring to a boil; cover and simmer for 20 minutes.

Add chilies, vinegar, and pepper; simmer for another 20 minutes. Stir in potato starch and cook for a few minutes until the soup is thickened.

Makes 8 servings.

*Note: Corn is a common allergen. We recommend a delayed food allergy test before trying this recipe.*

# Roasted Carrot Ginger Soup

*10 carrots*
*4 tbsp water*
*Sea Salt*
*4 c. vegetable stock*
*1½ tbsp ginger, grated*
*2 shallots, minced*
*2 garlic cloves, minced*
*Fresh ground pepper*

Clean the carrots then slice into rounds. On a baking sheet, arrange the carrots and toss with salt and 1 tbsp water. Broil for 8 minutes. Toss and broil another 20 mins. Meanwhile in a pot boil ginger and vegetable stock. Simmer for 15 mins. Mince the garlic and shallots. Pour remaining water into a large pot and add in the shallots and garlic sautéing until brown. Add the carrots from the oven, the vegetable stock and the onions to the pot. Boil for 10 minutes until soft. Puree the soup in a blender. Garnish with black pepper.

# Eggplant Bean Soup

*1 chopped onion*
*1 c. cooked brown rice*
*1 spear fresh broccoli, sliced*
*1 sliced zucchini*
*1 fresh yellow crookneck squash*
*½ c. diced eggplant*
*½ c. each: black-eyed peas, pink beans,
    white beans, red beans, and black beans*

Soak overnight black-eyed peas, pink beans, white beans, red beans, and black beans. Drain water off the next morning.

In a large crockpot simmer beans in 6 cups of water. Season with garlic and onion powder. About 6 hours later, add remaining ingredients and simmer another 45 minutes to cook and add fresh chopped parsley last. Ready to serve and enjoy anytime.

# Spicy Potato Cabbage Soup

*6 c. vegetable broth*
*2 lg potatoes, peeled and cubed*
*6-8 stalks celery, cut into ½-inch slices*
*10 fresh mushrooms, sliced*
*½ head cabbage, shredded*
*3-4 tsp Mrs. Dash extra spicy*
*3-4 tsp garlic powder*

Combine all ingredients in a large pot. Cook on low to medium heat 15-25 minutes or until potatoes are tender. Seasoning can be adjusted to taste as it is very spicy.

# Mediterranean Broccoli and Mushroom Soup

*1 med onion, chopped*
*½ c. buckwheat*
*2 cloves garlic, minced*
*2½-3 c. chopped broccoli*
*½ lb chopped mushrooms*
*1 sm turnip, peeled and chopped*
*1 (8 oz) can imported plum tomatoes
    (with liquid), chopped*
*3 tbsp minced fresh parsley*
*1 tsp paprika*
*1 tsp dried marjoram*
*½ tsp basil*
*¼ tsp dried rosemary*
*2 bay leaves*
*Freshly ground pepper to taste*
*¼ c. dry red wine*

Place first 4 ingredients in large pot and cover with 2 cups water or vegetable stock. Bring to boil, cover and simmer over low heat for 10 minutes. Add remaining ingredients to pot along with an additional 2½ cups water or stock. Cover and simmer over low heat for about 35 minutes or until vegetables and buckwheat are tender. Ideally this soup should stand an hour before serving. Serves 6-8.

# Lemongrass Soup

*5 c. lite coconut milk*
*3 c. broccoli, cut into bite-size pieces*
*3 tbsp dried lemon grass*
*3 green onions, finely chopped*
*2 tbsp coriander leaves, chopped*
*4 fresh serrano chilies*
*Juice of 2 limes*

In a saucepan, bring the coconut milk to a boil. Add the broccoli pieces and lemon grass. Reduce heat and simmer until the broccoli is tender, about 15 minutes. Do not cover. When the broccoli is tender, add the green onions coriander leaves, and chilies. Bring the heat up just below boiling. Remove the pan from heat and stir in the lime juice. Serve.

Makes 6 servings.

# Onion Leek Soup

*2 onions, sliced into rings*
*2 leeks, sliced (white and light green)*
*12 green onions, sliced*
*¼ c. minced shallots*
*2 cloves garlic, crushed*
*2 tsp grated fresh ginger root*
*1/16 tsp cayenne pepper*
*2 tsp all-purpose gluten-free*
  *baking flour or brown rice flour*
*Fresh ground pepper*
*Fresh chives, snipped*
*2 tsp lemon juice*
*7 c. water*
*1 c. white wine or use water*

Sauté onions in ½ cup water for 5 minutes. Add leeks, green onions, and shallots with another ½ cup water. Sauté a few minutes to soften. Add garlic, ginger, and cayenne. Stir in few times, then add flour and stir for a couple of minutes. Slowly mix in water and wine. Bring to boil, reduce heat, cover and simmer for 45 minutes. Add lemon juice and several twists of ground pepper. Mix. Ladle into bowls and garnish with snipped chives.

Serves 6 to 8.

# Red Lentil Coconut Soup

*2 c. red split lentils*
*1 onion, chopped*
*1 red bell pepper, diced*
*1 fresh jalapeno or serrano chili, chopped, including seeds*
*1 tbsp ginger, minced*
*2 garlic cloves, chopped*
*1 tbsp curry powder*
*½ tsp cinnamon*
*2 tsp salt*
*1/3 c. tomato paste*
*7 c. water*
*1 can light unsweetened coconut milk*
*1 (15 oz) can of chickpeas*
*1 tbsp freshly squeezed lime juice*
*Fresh cilantro, and lime wedges for serving*
*1 tbsp vegetable broth*

Heat 1 tbsp of vegetable broth in a large soup pot. Add in the jalapeno, bell pepper, and onions. Cook for 7 minutes. Add the tomato paste, spices, ginger and garlic. Cook for 3 mins. Fold in the chickpeas, lentils, coconut milk and water and cook for 25 more minutes. Garnish with lime juice, salt and cilantro.

# Coconut Milk Potato Salad

*2 lg potatoes, boiled and sliced*
*1 c. carrots, sliced into ¼-inch pieces*
*1 c. fresh green beans, sliced into 1-inch pieces*
*1 c. cauliflower flowerettes*
*1 c. sliced cabbage*
*¼ lb bean sprouts*
*1 cucumber, sliced*

## Sauce:

*¾ c. pecans*
*¾ c. almonds*
*¼ c. chopped onion*
*4 garlic cloves, minced*
*2 tsp crushed red pepper*
*1 tsp ground ginger*
*¼ tsp ground cumin*
*1½ c. coconut milk*
*3 tbsp fresh lemon juice*
*4 tbsp raw coconut aminos*

Blanch beans, carrots, cabbage, and cauliflower separately in water for 3 minutes each. Drain vegetables and arrange on platter. Top with bean sprouts and surround with cucumber and potato slices. Serve from platter topping each plate with sauce.

Serves 3

# Italian Kale

*2 lbs kale*
*1 garlic clove*
*1 onion*
*1 tsp ground cumin*
*1 c. tomatoes, chopped*
*½ c. tomato paste*
*½ c. peas*
*Sea salt*

Wash kale and steam. Saute garlic and onion in a saucepan with water. Once the onion is soft, add cumin, the tomato paste, tomatoes, peas and kale. Cook until tender. Garnish with sea salt to taste.

Serves 4

# Twice Baked Potatoes

*4 baking potatoes*
*2 egg whites or egg substitute*
*1 tbsp thyme*
*2 tbsp finely chopped onion*

Bake potatoes 50 minutes at 400 degrees. Slice lengthwise in halves. Scoop out pulp into mixing bowl; beat potato pulp with remaining ingredients. Return mixture to potato shells; top with paprika and bake 15 minutes at 350 degrees.

Serves 6 to 8

# Orange Sweet Potatoes

*4 med sweet potatoes*
*½ tsp grated orange rind*
*½ c. orange juice*
*2 tbsp apple juice*
*¼ tsp cinnamon*

Steam potatoes and peel. Mash all ingredients together. Bake in casserole dish, covered, for 25 minutes at 350 degrees.

Serves 4

# Kale, Tomato, Garlic and Thyme Pasta

*3 tbsp rice vinegar or balsamic vinegar*
*2 cloves garlic*
*2 c. cherry tomatoes*
*1½ tsp fresh thyme leaves*
*1 lb boiled, chopped kale leaves*
*Coarse salt and ground pepper*
*Gluten-free pasta noodles*

Cook pasta noodles as directed on package. In a large skillet, heat 1 tablespoon vinegar over medium heat. Add garlic cloves, thinly sliced, and cook, stirring until fragrant, 30 seconds. Add cherry tomatoes, quartered and fresh thyme leaves. Cook until tomatoes begin to break down, 2 minutes. Add kale and cook until heated through, 2 minutes. Season with salt and pepper. Drizzle with 2 teaspoons vinegar. Toss with gluten-free pasta noodles.

# Thai "Chicken" Enchiladas

*8 brown rice tortillas*
*14 oz almond tofu*
*1 tbsp raw coconut aminos*
*½ sweet onion, chopped*
*1/3 c. shredded carrots*
*½ c. shredded cabbage*
*4 garlic cloves, minced*
*½ tsp sea salt*
*½ tsp pepper*
*4 green onions, sliced*
*1/3 c. crushed cashews, and a handful for garnish*
*¼ c. chopped fresh cilantro, and a handful for garnish*
*2½ c. light coconut milk*
*2/3 c. sweet chili sauce*

Set oven at 350. Heat liquid aminos over a large skillet on medium heat. Add in ¼ tsp salt, garlic, carrots, cabbage & onions. Cook 8 mins. Fold in salt, pepper, cilantro, cashews, green onions & tofu. Cook for 2 mins. Fold in 1/3 cup chili sauce and ¾ cup coconut milk. Remove from heat. Whisk remaining chili sauce and coconut milk. Pour ½ cup in a 9x13 in a baking dish. Add in one tortilla. Scoop the tofu mixture inside and roll tightly. Do this until tortillas and tofu mixture are gone. Cover the tortillas with the rest of the coconut and chili sauce. Bake 20 mins. Garnish with cilantro and cashews.

## Butternut Squash with Coconut Milk Rice

*1¼ c. vegetable broth*
*1 c. light coconut milk*
*1 c. brown rice*
*1 c. finely chopped onion*
*2 stalks lemongrass, finely chopped*
*1¾ c. cubed peeled butternut squash*
*1 tsp chopped fresh thyme*
*Salt and pepper*
*1½ c. cooked black beans*
*1 tbsp lime juice*
*1 lime, zest and juice*

Bring coconut milk and broth to a boil. Throw in rice and simmer 20 mins. Remove from the heat. Saute an onion and lemongrass in a skillet with 1 tbsp lime juice until browned. Reduce to medium heat and throw in the squash. Cook 12 mins. Add in black beans, thyme salt and pepper. Cook 3 more mins. Add squash mixture to the rice. Garnish with lime juice and zest.

# Hummus and Avocado Toast with Roasted Tomatoes

*6-8 slices of gluten-free bread.*
*½ c. hummus*
*1 avocado*
*4 plum tomatoes, halved lengthwise, cores*
*   and seeds removed*
*3 tbsp balsamic vinegar*
*Sea salt & pepper to taste*

Set oven at 450. On a baking sheet, arrange the tomatoes. Sprinkle with vinegar, sea salt and pepper. Roast for 30 mins. Meanwhile toast the bread. Cut circles in the toast using a cookie cutter the same size as your tomato halves. Spread the hummus on each toast circle. Mash avocado and layer on top of the hummus. Sprinkle with sea salt & pepper. Top with a roasted tomato. Serve.

## Pumpkin Mac 'n Cheese Sauce

*1 tbsp avocado*
*1 tbsp arrowroot powder*
*¾ c. unsweetened almond milk*
*¼ tsp garlic powder*
*2 tsp Dijon mustard*
*1 c. canned pumpkin*
*Sea salt & pepper to taste*
*Sage, cinnamon, to taste*

Mix avocado and 1 tsp water in a pan over medium heat. Meanwhile, in a bowl mix together garlic powder, arrowroot and almond milk. Add to pan and whisk. Add in salt, pepper and Dijon. Cook on low 7 minutes. Fold in 1 cup pumpkin stirring until thick. Serve with gluten free macaroni noodles.

Serves 2

## Cauliflower Mashed Potatoes

*1 1/2 pounds cauliflower, cut into*
*  large pieces*
*3 garlic cloves, peeled*
*2 (14oz) cans low-sodium vegetable broth*
*Sea Salt*
*Freshly ground black pepper*
*2 tbsp fresh chives, chopped*

Combine broth, garlic and cauliflower in a large pan making sure that there is enough broth to cover cauliflower. Boil. Then simmer on medium heat for 12 minutes. Set aside 2 tbsp of the cooking broth, then drain the garlic and cauliflower. In a blender, process the garlic and cauliflower and 2 tbsp of cooking broth until smooth. Season with sea salt and pepper. Garnish with chives. Goes well with Mushroom Gravy or Oil Free Gravy from the sauces section of this book.

Serves 4.

# Orange Ginger Jackfruit and Brown Rice Salad with Orange Balsamic Vinaigrette

*About ¼ c. orange juice, divided into multiple uses*
*¾ c. jackfruit, cubed & cooked*
*1½ c. cooked brown rice*
*3½-4 c. diced celery, green bell peppers, jicama, radishes, carrots,*
*broccoli, red cabbage, green cabbage (mixed together)*
*1 tsp ground ginger*
*1 tsp cumin*
*Sea Salt*
*Black Pepper*
*Curry*
*Garlic*
*Onion powder*
*1 half orange*

Heat 1 tbsp of orange juice in a skillet. Once hot, sear the jackfruit for 3 mins. Set aside the jackfruit in a large bowl. Add 1 tbsp orange juice to the skillet. Stir in the cooked brown rice and warm for 2 mins. Add the rice to the bowl with the jackfruit. Add 2 tbsp orange juice to the skillet with the onion powder, garlic, curry, ginger, diced vegetables, cumin, salt and pepper. Stir to coat the vegetables. Cook over medium-high heat for 5 minutes. Add the vegetables to the large bowl. Slice the orange and use as garnish.

Serves 4.

# Mango Pineapple Bean-Stuffed Potatoes

## Spicy Black Beans

*2 garlic cloves, minced*
*1 c. red onion, chopped*
*1½ c. black beans*
*1 tsp chili powder*
*1 tsp cumin,*
*½ tsp coriander*
*½ tsp oregano*
*½ tsp paprika*
*1 tbsp lime juice*
*¼ c. water*
*Sea Salt*

Add 1 tsp of water to a skillet and heat. Add garlic and sauté for 3 mins. Meanwhile, set aside 2 tbsp raw red onions for garnish. Saute the rest of the onions until translucent, about 4 mins. Add in 1/4 cup water, lime juice, paprika, oregano, chili powder, cumin and black beans. Stir well until flavors meld and liquid is reduced. Add sea salt. Serve.

## Mango Pineapple Salsa

*1 mango, chopped*
*1 c. pineapple, chopped*
*2 tbsp cilantro, chopped*
*2 tbsp lime juice*
*1/8 tsp cayenne*
*½ tsp chili powder*
*Sea Salt*
*Combine all ingredients together &*
*refrigerate for 1 hour to let flavors meld.*

## Stuffed Potato

*Mango Pineapple Salsa Sweet*
*Potatoes*
*Spicy Black Beans*
*Avocado, diced*

Set oven to 450. Poke holes in potatoes with a fork. Bake potatoes for 45 mins the middle rack. Slice potatoes in half lengthwise. Scoop out the potato centers creating a bowl. Fill the bowls with the black bean mixture. Put on a baking sheet and bake for 15 mins. Remove and top with avocado and salsa. Serve.

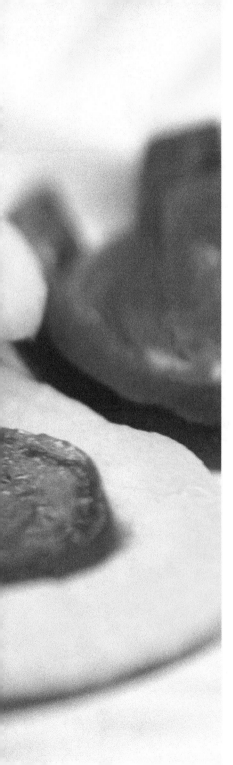

## Rustic Beet Tart

*6 sm beets, peeled*
*White wine*
*Fresh thyme sprigs*
*Salt*
*Pepper*
*1 sheet of gluten free flatbread*
*1½ c. prepared cashew ricotta ( see below)*
*Orange zest*
*Chopped walnuts*
*Chopped fresh basil*

Set oven to 400. Slice the beets into thin rounds. Coat them with thyme, wine and salt and pepper. Lay the slices on a foil lined baking sheet. Bake 10 mins. Place the flatbread onto a baking sheet. Spread on all of the cashew ricotta. Then top with the beet slices. Bake 30 mins at 350. Let cool. Garnish with basil, herbs, walnuts and lemon zest.

## Vegan Cashew Ricotta

*1 c soaked cashews*
*1 clove garlic*
*1 1/2 Tbsp lemon juice*
*1/4 cup almond milk*
*1/2 Tbsp dried Herbs de Provence*
*1/2 Tbsp agave*
*Orange zest*
*1/2 tsp black pepper*
*Sea salt*

In a blender, add all ingredients and blend until smooth.

# Vegan Spicy Lasagna with Green Basil Pesto

*1 box no-boil gluten free lasagna pasta strips*
*14 oz almond tofu*
*1-2 c. of shredded vegan mozzarella or Jack cheese*

### Fillings:
*2 c. zucchini, thinly sliced*
*5 cloves garlic, chopped*
*1½ c. mushrooms, sliced*
*coconut nectar*
*lemon juice*

### Garnish:
*Crushed red pepper flakes*
*Fresh basil*
*Parsley, chopped*

### Pesto:
*2 c. raw pine nuts*
*½ c. garlic*
*1 c. parsley, chopped*
*1 bunch fresh basil*
*2 lemons, squeezed*
*2 tbsp liquid Stevia*
*1 tsp pepper*
*1 tsp sea salt*
*1 jalapeno, stem removed*

Prepare pesto sauce. In a skillet, toast pine nuts for 1 min. with a tsp of water and pinch of salt. Combine all of pesto ingredients, including pine nuts to a blender until smooth. Set aside. In a casserole dish, place a thin layer of tomatoes, pasta strips, then pesto, then vegan cheese, then more pasta strips and finally a layer of vegan mozzarella. Set aside. Slice tofu into strips. In a pan, sauté the tofu in the coconut nectar and lemon juice. Cover and heat for 4 mins browning the tofu edges. Top with sea salt and pepper. Set aside. In the pan, add in lemon juice, pine nuts, garlic cloves, zucchini, mushrooms and a pinch of salt and pepper. Saute until the zucchini is browned and mushrooms are cooked through. Remove and set aside. In the casserole dish, spread a layer of zucchini, then pasta, then tofu, then mushrooms, then zucchini again, then pasta again. Do this until ingredients are gone. Top it all with vegan cheese and pesto sauce. Cover and bake at 350 for 45 mins. Then, broil for 5 mins to brown the top layer of cheese. Garnish with red pepper, parsley and basil.

# Red Quinoa Medley

*1 c. red quinoa*
*1 butternut squash, peeled and diced*
*½ c. cranberries, halved*
*½ red onion, diced*
*1 clove garlic, minced*
*balsamic vinegar*
*liquid Stevia to taste*
*sea salt*
*black pepper*
*1 tsp ginger*
*½ cup chopped pecans*
*2 tbsp chopped parsley*

Set oven to 375. Cook the red quinoa according to instructions. Put the garlic, onion, cranberries, squash, drizzle of vinegar, 1 tsp stevia, sea salt, ginger and curry in a medium pan. Roast in the oven for 20 mins until the squash is tender. Meanwhile, toast the pecans in a skillet. In a serving bowl, add in the squash mixture, quinoa, toasted pecans and parsley. Drizzle with vinegar and toss.

# Quinoa Stuffed Portobello Mushrooms

*1 Portobello mushroom per person*
*Balsamic vinegar*
*Sea salt to taste*
*Ground pepper to taste*

## Stuffing:

*4 cloves chopped garlic*
*1/2 cup of cooked quinoa per mushroom cap*
*Handful of cherry tomatoes halved*
*1 scallion per mushroom, sliced*
*A sprinkle of raisins*

*A sprinkle of toasted pine nuts*

*Fresh chopped parsley, basil or mint*

Set oven to 350. Grease baking dish with vinegar. Place the mushroom caps in the baking dish and drizzle with more balsamic vinegar. Sprinkle with sea salt & pepper. Bake for 15 mins. Meanwhile sauté the garlic in a skillet with a tsp vinegar. Add in the pine nuts, raisins, scallions, tomatoes and quinoa. Season with sea salt and pepper. Garnish with herbs. Stuff each mushroom with mixture and then bake for 20 mins covered.

# Veggie Gyros

*2 pieces of gluten-free round flat-bread*
*6 gluten free falafel balls*
*1 onion, sliced*
*½ c. rice vinegar (for various uses)*
*Pepper*
*1 tomato, sliced*
*½ avocado, sliced – tossed in lemon juice*
*2 dill pickles*
*Tahini sauce*
*2 tbsp harissa (for the gyro sauce)*


Toss the sliced onions in ¼ cup vinegar. Brush the flatbread with vinegar and grill until crisp. Grill the falafel to warm.  Put the falafel, onions, avocado, pickels tomato and harissa sauce and tahini in the flatbread and enjoy.

Serves 2.

# Avocado Spinach Egg Salad Sandwiches

*2 c. egg whites or substitute, cooked*
*4 oz plain coconut milk yogurt*
*2 avocados*
*1 stalk celery, chopped*
*1 c. baby spinach*
*Hot pepper flakes to taste*
*Your choice of gluten free bread, toasted*

Mash up the cooked eggs with coconut milk yogurt. Sprinkle with sea salt and pepper. Mash up the avocados and season with sea salt and pepper. Combine the egg and avocado mixtures.  Add in spinach, celery and hot pepper flakes. Spread on your gluten-free bread.

Serves 6.

# Vegan Nachos

## Black Beans:
*1½ c. soaked dried black beans (soak overnight)*
*1 c. vegetable broth*
*¼ c. onion*
*1 tsp chipotle*
*1 tsp chili powder*
*1 tsp onion*
*cilantro*
*bell pepper*
*2 cloves garlic, chopped*

Simmer the beans with all of the above ingredients until tender.

## Additional Ingredients:
*Raw flaxseed chips or lentil chips*
*Cheese (vegan, pepperjack, nacho flavor)*
*Jalapeño*
*Avocado*
*Onion*
*Olives*
*Tomato*
*Cilantro*
*Almond Tofu Taco Crumbles (see tofu taco recipe)*

*Additional ingredients and instructions continued on Page 194*

# Cashew Sour Cream

*1 cup cashews, soaked overnight and drained*
*1/2 cup almond tofu*
*1-2 tsp agave or 6 drops liquid stevia*
*2 Tbsp lemon juice*
*Lemon zest*
*3/4 tsp sea salt*
*1/3 cup water*
*garlic powder*
*pepper*
*chipotle*
*chili salt*
*2 Tbsp almond milk*

Add all sour cream ingredients in a blender.
Blend until smooth.  Layer all nacho ingredients.
Enjoy!

Serves 6.

# Vegan Mexi Lettuce Wraps

*1 bunch romaine hearts*
*1 sweet potato, diced*
*1 can black beans, drained*
*4 radishes, sliced*
*10 cherry tomatoes, halved*
*½ c. cilantro, chopped*
*Juice of 1 lime*
*5 tbsp raw coconut aminos, for various uses*
*Sea Salt*
*Black Pepper*
*1 tbsp cumin*
*1 tbsp chili powder*
*1 avocado, diced*

Using 2 tbsp liquid aminos, sauté sweet potatoes, chili powder, cumin, sea salt and pepper in a skillet for 10 mins until browned. In a bowl, mix the beans, potatoes, tomatoes, radishes, 3 tbsp liquid aminos, lime juice, cilantro and salt and pepper. Mix well. Scoop into each romaine lettuce wrap. Garnish with avocado and cilantro.

Serves 10.

# Vegetable Quinoa Paella

1 onion, chopped
3 cloves garlic, minced
1½ c. quinoa
¼ tsp saffron, crushed
2 tsp smoked paprika
½ tsp ground cumin

Dash cayenne
1 can diced tomatoes
1 red bell pepper, chopped
1 can red kidney beans, drained
2¾–3 c. vegetable broth
2 med zucchini, sliced
1 c. peas
1 can artichoke hearts, quartered

Rinse the quinoa. Drain and set aside. Saute the garlic and onion in a skillet with 1 tsp water until browned. Mix in the saffron and quinoa. Cook 3 mins. Add the beans, paprika, cumin, cayenne, peppers, tomatoes and vegetable broth. Boil, then cook on low covered for 25 mins. Stir in zucchini and cover. Cook 5 mins until quinoa is done. Stir in the peas and cook until liquid is dissolved. Garnish with artichoke hearts.

Serves 5.

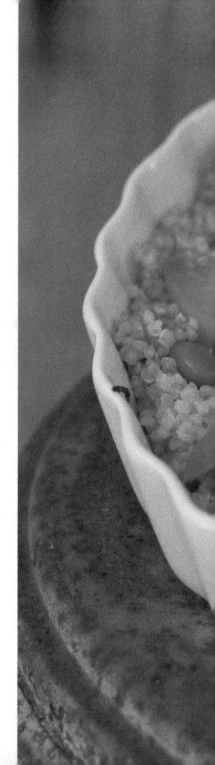

# Raw Pad Thai

## Sauce:

2 cups coconut meat
1 ½ cups water
1/4 tsp. ground lime leaf
1/2 cup fresh thai basil
1 tbsp avocado
1/2 cup coconut syrup
2 tsp. paprika
1 1/2 tsp. cayenne
1 ½ tsp. sea salt
1 tsp. garlic powder
1 lime juice

## Other ingredients:

1 c red pepper, sliced
1 ½ c broccoli, chopped
3 carrots, peeled & sliced
6 zucchinis
1/2 cup fresh basil
1/2 cup cashews, crushed

Use a spirooli to make zucchini noodles. Set aside. Blend all of the sauce ingredients until smooth. Mix the noodles in a large bowl with the chipped veggies. Garnish with cashews. Serves 2.

# DESSERTS...

## Banana Split Bites

*3 bananas*
*1/2 gallon of non-dairy coconut ice cream*
*1/2 cup chopped nuts*
*1 cup of non-dairy chocolate, melted*
*Non-dairy whipped cream (use cashew cream recipe in this book)*
*Cherries*

Cut the bananas into thirds. Scoop out a pocket in each banana. Fill it with ice cream. Dip the bottom of the banana into melted chocolate. Freeze until serving time. Top with whipped cream and fresh cherries.

## Apple Oatmeal Cookies

½ c. unsweetened applesauce
1 c. unpasteurized apple juice
1 egg white or egg substitute
1 tsp vanilla extract
3 c. gluten free oats
½ c. brown rice flour
½ c. gluten free oat bran
½ tsp baking soda
1/3 c. chopped nuts and/or raisins

Combine all ingredients in mixing bowl, blend well. Drop by rounded teaspoons onto cookie sheets sprayed with non-stick spray. Bake at 350 degrees for 12-15 minutes. Serves 24.

## Oatmeal Cookies

½ c. prepared almond butter
1 c. unpasteurized apple juice
1 egg white or egg substitute
1 tsp pure vanilla extract
½ tsp baking soda
3 c. gluten free oats
1 c. gluten-free or brown rice flour
1/3 c. chopped nuts and/or raisins

Combine all ingredients in a mixing bowl and mix well. Drop rounded teaspoons onto sprayed (non-stick spray) cookie sheets. Bake at 350 degrees for 12-15 minutes. No cholesterol and no sugar!

## Banana Cookies

1 c. banana puree (2 med bananas)
½ c. date pieces
¼ c. chopped almonds
1 tsp vanilla
1½ c. uncooked gluten free oatmeal

Pour banana puree into a bowl and add remaining ingredients. Mix well; drop by tablespoons onto a non-stick cookie sheet (use non-stick spray). Bake at 375 degrees for 20 minutes. Makes 2 dozen.

## Banana Raisin Cookies

1¼ c. gluten free rolled oats
1 c. gluten-free baking flour
  or brown rice flour
1 tsp cinnamon
½ c. apple juice
2 ripe bananas, mashed
¾ c. raisins
1 tsp vanilla

Preheat oven to 350 degrees. Combine all dry ingredients in a large bowl. Add remaining ingredients; mix well. Batter should be a little stiff. Drop by teaspoons onto non-stick cookie sheet and flatten slightly. Bake for 15 minutes. Makes 15-18 cookies.

## Harvest Apple Cookies

*1¼ c. gluten-free flour*
*1 tsp Rumford baking powder*
*½ tsp cinnamon*
*½ c. almond butter*
*¼ c. unsweetened applesauce*
*½ c. unpasteurized apple juice*
*½ c. chopped dates or date nuggets*
*1 c. apple, chopped and peeled*
*½ c. gluten free rolled oats*
*¼ c. gluten free oat bran*

Preheat oven to 350 degrees. Combine dry ingredients; mix wet ingredients into dry. Mix batter until smooth. Drop by teaspoons onto non-stick cookie sheet sprayed with cookie spray. Bake 15-20 minutes until lightly browned. Makes 24.

## Soft Pumpkin Cookies

*1¾ c. all-purpose gluten-free baking flour*
 *or brown rice flour*
*¼ c. gluten free oat bran*
*1 tbsp non-aluminum gluten free baking powder*
*1 tsp cinnamon*
*½ tsp nutmeg*
*2/3 c. chopped nuts (optional)*
*2/3 c. sunflower seeds (raw, optional)*
*½ c. raisins*
*½ c. unfiltered apple juice*
*½ c. unsweetened applesauce*
*1½ c. mashed pumpkin*

Preheat oven to 350 degrees. Combine dry ingredients in order given. Mix wet ingredients well and add to dry ingredients. Stir batter until well blended. Drop by tablespoon onto non-stick cookie sheets sprayed with non-stick spray. Bake 10-12 minutes until firm and lightly browned. Makes 2 dozen.

# Carob Brownies

*2 egg whites or egg substitute*
*1 tbsp honey*
*1½ tsp vanilla extract*
*1 c. grated zucchini*
*3 tbsp dairy/whey-free carob powder*
*½ c. gluten free oat bran*
*½ c. apple juice*
*½ c. chopped dates*

Beat eggs, honey and vanilla for 1 minute. Slowly while beating, add remaining ingredients. Bake in a non-stick 9-inch square pan (use non-stick spray) for 30 minutes at 350 degrees. Serves 8 to 10.

# Raisin Chews

*3 egg whites or egg substitute, beaten slightly*
*12 oz frozen apple juice*
*¼ tsp cloves*
*3 tsp coriander*
*1 c. granola*
*1 c. gluten free oatmeal*
*2 c. raisins*
*1 tsp allspice*
*3 tsp anise*
*½ tsp vanilla*
*2 c. gluten-free baking flour or*
*  brown rice flour*
*½ c. gluten free oat bran*

Preheat oven to 350 degrees. Combine the above list of ingredients in a mixing bowl. If mixture is too wet to form drop cookies, add oatmeal (can add more oatmeal if needed). Drop by spoonfuls onto ungreased cookie sheet. Bake at 350 degrees for 5-10 minutes or until cookies start to spring back when you touch them. Makes about 50 cookies.

# Crunchy Carrot Cake

*2/3 c. egg substitutes, whipped*
*1 c. grated carrots*
*1 (20 oz) can crushed pineapple, in its own juice*
*1 tsp baking soda*
*1 tsp cinnamon*
*1 c. unfiltered apple juice*
*1 c. gluten free oat bran*
*1 c. gluten-free pastry flour*
*½ c. raisins*
*½ c. chopped walnuts*

Combine dry ingredients together. Combine liquid ingredients together. Blend together; mix well. Pour into non-stick baking dish. Bake at 350 degrees for 45 minutes. Serves 15.

# Carrot Cake Frosting

In a saucepan, cook and stir 1 cup apple juice and 3 teaspoons tapioca until thickened. When cooked, add 1 teaspoon vanilla. Spread frosting on cake and serve.

## Date Cake

*2/3 c. egg substitutes*
*1/3 c. honey or apple juice*
*1 tsp baking soda*
*½ c. grated carrots (2 small carrots)*
*1 c. grated zucchini (1 small)*
*1 tsp cinnamon*
*1 c. water*
*1 c. gluten free oat bran*
*1 c. gluten-free pastry flour*
*1 c. date pieces*

Combine together in the order given: Blend with hand mixer. Pour into cake pan sprayed with non-stick cooking spray. Bake in pre-heated 350 degree oven, 30 minutes. When the cake reaches warm or room temperature, frost with **Date Frosting**. Please see next recipe. This outstandingly delicious cake can be served at warm or at room temperature. Serves 15.

## Date Frosting

*1 c. apple juice*
*½ c. date pieces*
*1 tsp vanilla*
*3 tbsp tapioca granules*

Place all ingredients in blender and process for 2 minutes. Cook in saucepan 5 minutes over low heat, stirring constantly. Cool down to a warm temperature and frost cake. This delicious frosting can be served at room temperature not only on the date cake but also on any cake of our choice.

# Fruitcake

2 c. coarsely chopped dried figs
2 c. chopped dried apricots
½ c. chopped candied lemon rind
1½ c. golden raisins
1½ c. chopped dates
2 c. chopped pecans
2/3 c. green candied cherries, halved
2/3 c. red candied cherries, halved
½ tsp gluten free baking soda
1½ c.  gluten-free baking
  flour or brown rice flour

¾ tsp nutmeg
½ tsp cinnamon
½ tsp ground cloves
½ tsp ground cardamom
2 tbsp almond butter
12 egg whites or egg substiute
1½ c. apple juice
2 tbsp water
1 tsp Rumford baking powder
1 c. red wine
Brandy

In a large bowl, combine the figs, apricots, lemon peel, raisins, dates, pecans and cherries.  In another bowl, sift together the flours (there should be a total of 3 cups of flour, either all brown rice flour, or a combination of all-purpose flour and brown rice flour), baking powder, spices and almond butter. Add the flour mixture to the fruit and toss together until all the bits of fruit are separated and coated. Beat the eggs with the apple juice. Stir in the wine. Dissolve the baking soda in the water and stir it in too. Combine the egg mixture with the flour and fruit mixture and thoroughly stir them together. Pour into 6 medium-small (7½ x 3½-inch) loaf pans. Bake the cakes in a preheated oven at 275 degrees for 2 hours. Allow the cakes to cool and remove them from the pans. Wrap each cake in several layers of cheese cloth and soak the cloth with as much brandy as it will absorb. Wrap the cake again, in foil or plastic wrap, to retain the moisture. To allow the fruit cakes to develop their full flavor, store them in a cool place for 4 weeks. Makes 6 medium-sized fruitcakes.

# Coffee Cake with Streusel Topping

1 c. raisins
4½ c. all-purpose gluten-free baking flour
   or brown rice flour
2 tbsp baking powder
1½ tbsp carob powder
2 tsp cinnamon
½ tsp cardamom
½ tsp nutmeg
4 egg whites or egg substitute
2 lg bananas, mashed
10 oz frozen apple juice
1 tbsp vanilla
3 tbsp mineral water
¾ c. water
3 tbsp dry sherry (optional)

## *Streusel Topping:*

1 c. granola
2 tbsp frozen apple juice
1 tsp vanilla extract
½ tsp cinnamon
¼ tsp nutmeg
½ tsp cardamom

Process granola in the blender just long enough to reduce the coarseness of the cereal. Add the other topping ingredients and sprinkle on the cake.

Cover raisins with hot water to soak. In a large bowl, sift together the flour, baking powder, carob powder, and spices. Mix together the remaining ingredients, except the eggs. Stir this mixture into dry ingredients. Beat the eggs until stiff peaks form and fold them into the batter. Add the drained raisins and stir well. Pour the batter into a large nonstick baking pan. Sprinkle streusel topping evenly over the cake. Bake in a preheated 350 degree oven for 50-60 minutes. Cool.

Serves 9

# Blueberry Cake

6 c. apple juice
1 tsp lemon rind
1 tsp vanilla
2 c. quinoa
1 pint blueberries

Bring first 3 ingredients to a boil in a medium pan. Add quinoa; reduce heat and stir until almost thick, about 5 minutes. Add the blueberries to the hot mixture (berries will burst, leaving streaks and cake will be very colorful). Remove from heat. Rinse a 9 x 9-inch square glass baking dish with cold water. Pour mixture into pan and chill in refrigerator until set, about 45-60 minutes. Remove from refrigerator, place a serving platter over baking dish and turn upside down. Cut into squares. Can be garnished with chopped nuts or whipped almond tofu cream. Serves 10 to 15.

# Pumpkin Spice Cake

3 c. organic pumpkin mix
1 c. unpasteurized apple juice
½ c. raisins
2 c. all-purpose gluten-free baking flour or brown rice flour
1 tsp baking soda
1 tsp Rumford baking powder
2 tsp cinnamon
¼ tsp nutmeg
¼ tsp allspice
4 egg whites or egg substitute, whipped
1 tsp pure vanilla extract
1 c. granola
¼ c. honey or applesauce

Combine dry ingredients together. Combine wet ingredients together, and then blend both (mixing well). Pour into non-stick baking dish. Bake at 350 degrees for about 45 minutes. Serves 15.

# Apple Spice Cake

4 c. finely diced apples (5-6 apples)
½ c. frozen apple juice
½ c. water
½ c. raisins
2 1/2 c. all-purpose gluten-free baking flour or brown rice flour
1 c. granola
2½ tsp cinnamon
¼ tsp nutmeg
¼ tsp allspice
4 egg whites or egg substitute
1 tsp vanilla extract
2 tsp Rumford baking powder
2 tsp baking soda

Combine diced apples, apple juice, water and raisins in a bowl. Cover with plastic wrap; refrigerate 4-6 hours. Sift flours, baking powder, baking soda, cinnamon, nutmeg, and allspice into large bowl. Beat egg whites until peaks form; fold into flour mixture. Add apple raisin mixture (including juice). Add vanilla extract and granola. Stir well. Pour into non-stick bundt pan. 325 degrees for 1½ hours. Turn cake out of the pan onto large sheet of foil. Wrap completely in foil. Let sit for several hours. Servings: 12.

# Bananas in Coconut Milk

*5 bananas, quartered*
*1½ tsp coconut milk*
*½ tsp sea salt*
*2 tbsp apple juice*
*3 drops jasmine essence*
*2 tbsp roasted mung beans, crushed*

Boil all the ingredients (except the beans) in a saucepan. Then simmer 3 mins. Serve in a dessert dish warm or cold. Garnish with mung beans. Serves 5.

# Banana Pecan Pie

### *Pie Crust:*
*1½ c. granola*
*1-1/3 c. apple juice*
*1 tsp cinnamon*

Mix all ingredients in a pie pan to make a shell. Bake for 10 mins at 350.

### *Pie Filling:*
*1 pkg natural banana pudding mix*
*Handful of Pecans*
*2 bananas, sliced*
*½ c. apple juice*
*½ c. water*

Bring, liquids and pudding mix to a boil in a saucepan. Add bananas. Simmer 5 mins. Pour into pie crust. Garnish with pecans. Chill before serving.

# Banana Cream Pie

### *In Blender Add:*
*½ c tightly-packed cooked brown rice*
*1/3 c. apple juice*

Blend until thick and smooth.

### *Add:*
*2¼ c. water*
*1 tsp almond butter*
*5 tbsp unsweetened almond flour*
*¼ c. coconut aminos*

Continue to blend until thoroughly mixed. Pour contents of blender into saucepan. Bring to boil, stirring constantly. Remove from heat; allow to cool 15 minutes. Slice 2 large ripe bananas and stir into mixture. Pour into a pre-baked crust (use one of our crust recipes). Refrigerate for at least 2 hours. When ready to serve, top with banana slices and pecan halves. Makes 1 large 11-inch pie.

# Chocolate Banana Brownies

*Non-stick cooking spray*
*4 tbsp cocoa powder*
*¾ c. water*
*1 very ripe banana*
*1 c. pitted dates or apple juice*
*2 lg egg whites or egg substitute*
*1 tsp vanilla extract*
*1 tsp Rumford baking powder*
*¼ tsp sea salt*
*1 c. all-purpose gluten-free baking flour*
  *or brown rice flour*
*½ c. gluten free oat bran*

Preheat the oven to 350 degrees. Spray an 8-inch round or square cake pan with non-stick cooking spray.

Place the cocoa, ¼ cup water and the banana into a large blender or into the bowel of a food processor that has been fitted with a steel blade. Blend until it is smooth. Add pitted dates, eggs, vanilla extract, baking powder, and salt; blend until the mixture is smooth. Add the flour, oat bran, and ½ cup water (a little at a time) and blend again until smooth.

Pour the chocolate mixture into the prepared pan. Bake at 350 degrees for 20-25 minutes. Wait until the brownies have cooled to cut into servings. Store brownies in the refrigerator.

# Grilled Carob Banana Boats

*4 bananas*
*¼ c. carob chips*
*½ c. chopped strawberries*
*1/3 c. granola or gluten free graham crackers*
*½ c. vegan marshmallows*
*¼ c. chopped walnuts or pecans*

Preheat grill. Have each banana through the peel without cutting through to the bottom peel. Make space in in the bananas center for toppings. Fill each banana with all toppings. Fold foil around the bottom of each banana. Put on the grill and cook until toppings are melted, about 10 mins. Cool.

Serves 4.

# Pearadise Pie

*3½ c. granola*
*¼ c. toasted gluten-free bran*
*¼ c. almond butter*
*1 (12 oz) can pear nectar*
*1 tbsp unsweetened almond flour*
*1 tsp vanilla*
*Whole strawberries (optional)*
*2 tbsp lemon juice*
*1 tbsp water*
*2 small bananas*
*2 c. fresh strawberries, sliced*
*½ sm cantaloupe, seeded, sliced, and peeled*

## Pie Crust:

Crush granola into fine crumbs. Measure 1¼ cup crumbs. Combine with bran and almond butter. Press onto bottom and up sides of a 9-inch pie plate to form a firm, even crust. Bake in a 375 degree oven for 4-6 minutes. Cool on a wire rack.

## Glaze:

Combine nectar and flour. Cook and stir over medium heat until thickened and bubbly. Cook and stir 2 minutes longer. Stir in vanilla; set aside.

## To Assemble Pie:

In small bowl, combine lemon juice and water. Dip in banana and pear slices, being careful not to mash the banana. In crust, layer ¼ cup of the glaze, the banana slices, another ¼ cup of the glaze, the sliced strawberries and another ¼ cup of the glaze. Arrange the pear and cantaloupe slices atop. Top with the remaining glaze. Chill 2-4 hours. Makes 8 servings.

# Apricot Pie

For oat nut crust, blend in blender until a coarse meal:
*1½ c. rolled gluten free oats*

Mix in a bowl with:
*½ c. walnuts, chopped fine*
*¼ c. apple juice*
*¼ c. water*

Let stand 30 minutes. Oil a 9-inch pie pan and press mixture firmly into bottom and sides, using the back of a large spoon. Bake at 350 degrees for 30 minutes until edges begin to brown.

## Filling:

Snip into small pieces with scissors dipped in cold water:
*1 c. dried apricots*

Place apricots in saucepan; add:
*1½ c. apple juice*

## Also needed:
*2 tbsp kanten flakes*

Bring to a boil, reduce heat and simmer 15 minutes until fruit is soft. Sprinkle on top to dissolve: 2 tablespoons kanten flakes. Stir in and cook over medium heat, stirring 3 minutes. Set off heat to cool. When it begins to set, pour into baked pie shell. Chill. This dessert can be made the day before. Serves 8.

# Pineapple Upside-Down Cake

## Topping:
*6 slices canned pineapple rings*
*Pecan or walnut halves*
*2 tbsp almond butter*
*¼ c. honey*

## Cake:
*4 egg whites or egg substitute*
*2 tbsp pineapple juice*
*½ tsp gluten free baking powder*
*½ c. gluten-free all-purpose baking flour*
  *or brown rice flour*
*½ c. honey*

Set oven to 350. Line a cake pan with wax paper. Melt together in a saucepan, almond butter and honey. Spread over the wax paper. Arrange pineapple and nuts in the pan. For the cake mix the honey and juice. Sift the flour and baking powder over the mixture. Beat eggs and add into the cake mixture. Mix well. Spread batter over pineapple in pan. Bake 30 mins. Cool. Turn pan upside down and peel off wax paper.

# Crumb Topped Fruit Pie

## Crust:
1-1/3 c. gluten-free bread crumbs,
  mixed with 1/3 c. bran
1 tbsp each pectin and arrowroot
1 tsp coriander
½ tsp lemon extract
1 tsp vanilla extract

## Filling:
3 c. sliced fruit or berries of choice
1/3 c. frozen apple juice

## Topping:
1 c. fine gluten-free
  bread crumbs
1 tbsp cinnamon
1 tsp vanilla extract

## Crust:
Place ingredients in a bowl, mixing well. Using a rubber spatula, press the mixture into the non-stick pie pan firmly (bottom and sides) to form an even crust. Bake the crust at 350 degrees for 15 minutes, until lightly browned. Remove from oven and allow cooling.

## Filling:
Place filling ingredients in a saucepan. Bring to a boil, then lower the heat and simmer for a few minutes, stirring frequently until the mixture is thickened. Pour the fruit filling into the prepared crust. Combine the topping ingredients, mixing well. Sprinkle the topping over the filling, lightly pressing it in the fruit with a spatula. Bake at 375 degrees for 15 minutes. Let pie cool, and then slice to serve.

Serves 6 to 8.

# French Apple Pie

## *Crust:*
*2 c. granola*
*Cinnamon*
*1/3 c. apple juice*
*Additional water*

Mix ingredients into a large pie pan and press to form shell. Sprinkle with cinnamon.

## *Filling:*
*4 med Granny Smith apples, sliced*
*Cinnamon*
*2 tsp lemon juice*

Arrange sliced apples in shell. Sprinkle with lemon juice and cinnamon. Cover with foil and bake for 45 minutes at 350 degrees.

## *Glaze:*
*½ c. apple juice*
*1 tbsp unsweetened almond flour*
*½ c. water*

Combine flour and liquids in saucepan. Cook and stir until mixture thickens and becomes clear. Pour or spoon over pie. Chill.

# Sweet Potato Pie

*3 or 4 sweet potatoes, baked*
*1 (16 oz) can crushed pineapple, in own juice*
*¼ c. chopped nuts (pecans, walnuts, or almonds)*
*1/3 c. granola*
*1 tsp pure vanilla extract*
*½ tsp pumpkin pie spice*
*1/3 c. unsweetened coconut, shredded*

Spray a glass pie pan with non-stick spray. Peel sweet potatoes; dice and mash in a large mixing bowl. Add can of pineapple with juice, vanilla extract, and pumpkin pie spice. Beat thoroughly with mixer, whipping until smooth. Pour into the pie pan or any glass baking dish and top with coconut, chopped nuts and granola. Bake at 350 degrees for 25 minutes.

A natural delicious dessert with fiber and no sugar. Enjoy.

# Pineapple-Lemon Meringue Pie

## *Crust:*

1¼ c. gluten-free crumbs
3 tbsp frozen apple juice
1 tsp vanilla extract
1/8 tsp lemon extract

Place ingredients in a bowl, mixing well. Using a rubber spatula, press the mixture firmly into the non-stick pie pan (bottom and sides) to form an even crust. Bake crust at 350 degrees for 15 minutes, until lightly browned. Remove from oven and allow to cool.

## *Filling:*

1 (20 oz) can unsweetened pineapple
1-1/3 c. rice milk
½ c. frozen apple juice
3 tbsp lemon juice
2 tbsp frozen orange juice
2 tsp unflavored gelatin
2 tsp arrowroot
Dash of turmeric (for color)
1½ tsp lemon extract
1½ tsp vanilla extract
½ c. egg whites or egg substitute

Place the filling ingredients, except for the flavor extracts and egg whites, into a blender and blend at high speed for 5 minutes. Set a large strainer over a mixed bowl and pour mixture through strainer, discard residue in strainer (this insures a smooth pie filling). Transfer the filling mixture to a double boiler, cook for about 5 minutes, while stirring with a wire whisk until mixture is very hot. Stir in lemon, and vanilla extracts. Let filling cool slightly, and then pour into prepared crust. Beat egg whites until stiff peaks form. Swirl the beaten egg gently over the filling. Place the pie in the oven on a middle rack under a hot broiler. Watch meringue carefully, brown just lightly, and then remove from oven. Chill pie for several hours or overnight until firm.

# Pumpkin Pie

## *Crust:*

*1½ c. granola*
*1 tsp cinnamon*
*1/3 c. apple juice*

Mix above ingredients in a 9-inch pie pan. Press to form shell.

## *Filling:*

*¾ c. apple juice*
*¼ c. honey*
*½ tsp cinnamon*
*¾ tsp ginger*
*¼ tsp nutmeg*
*3 tbsp sweet dark rum*
*¼ tsp ground cloves*
*2 c. pureed cooked pumpkin*
*1 c. egg whites or egg substitute*
*3 tbsp crystallized ginger, chopped*
*1 tbsp Stevia as substitute*

In a bowl, combine the apple juice, honey, stevia, spices and pureed pumpkin. In another bowl beat the eggs with the rum. Combine the 2 mixtures and blend thoroughly. Sprinkle the crystallized ginger over the bottom of the pie crust. Carefully ladle the filling over the ginger. Bake the pies in the preheated 400 degree oven for 35-40 minutes or until a knife inserted comes out clean.

## Peach Cobbler

*1 c. pineapple juice*
*½ c. pitted dates*
*1 tsp vanilla*
*1 tsp cinnamon*
*1 tsp tapioca*
*3 c. mashed fresh peaches*
*1 tbsp almonds*
*½ c. pitted dates*
*1/3 c. gluten free oatmeal*

Blend first 5 ingredients. In a non-stick baking dish, layer peaches; pour juice mixture over. Grind remaining ingredients as topping and spoon over top. Bake at 350 degrees for 45 minutes.

Serves 6 to 8.

## Blueberry-Apple Crisp

*1 c. granola*
*1 c. toasted gluten free oats*
*¼ c. almond butter*
*¼-1/3 c. apple juice*

### *Filling:*
*3 apples, cored and sliced*
  *(or 1 can water-packed apples)*
*1 c. blueberries*
*½ c. apple juice*
*¼ c. unsweetened almond flour*

Combine crust ingredients and set aside. Combine filling ingredients in a bowl. Pour filling ingredients into a baking dish, sprinkle with crust ingredients. Bake at 350 degrees for 30 minutes
or until bubbly.

# Apricot Cobbler

2¾ c. mashed fresh apricots, pitted but not peeled
1 c. apple juice
1 tsp cinnamon
1/3 c. gluten free oatmeal
1/3 c. dates
½ tsp cinnamon
1 c. pitted dates

Spread apricots evenly on bottom of 6 x 10-inch baking dish. Pour apple juice in a blender and add dates. Puree, and then add 1 teaspoon cinnamon. Pour over apricots. Make topping by grinding oatmeal, dates, and ½ teaspoon cinnamon in blender.

# Peach or Pear Crisp

1 lg can peaches or pears, totally drained in colander
½ c. raisins
¼ - ½ c. chopped walnuts or pecans
¼ c. unsweetened coconut, shredded (optional)
½ tsp cinnamon
½ c. gluten free oats
½ c. granola
6 oz apple juice
½ tsp vanilla extract

In glass baking dish, sprayed with non-stick spray, spread fruit evenly, then sprinkle and continue layering all ingredients in order. Blend apple juice and vanilla and pour evenly over all. Bake at 350 degrees for 20 minutes.

# Cherry Cobbler

### Crust:
1½ c. granola
1/3 c. apple juice
1 tsp cinnamon

Mix above ingredients into 9-inch pie pan. Press to form shell.

### Filling:
3 c. frozen cherries
3 tsp unsweetened almond flour
2 tsp water
1 c. walnuts, chopped

Place cherries, water, and flour in saucepan. Mix well to dilute flour. Bring to boil, reduce flame to low, and simmer for 3-5 minutes. Stir to prevent lumping and sticking. Remove from flame and allow to cool. Add walnuts. Pour over crust in pie pan. Bake at 375 degrees for about 15 minutes. Serves 6.

# Sweet Potato Apple Casserole

*1 lb apples*
*1¼ lb sweet potatoes*
*2 tbsp unsweetened almond flour*
*4 tbsp water*
*1 c. apple juice*
*Cinnamon*

Bake or steam sweet potatoes until soft. Peel, slice and layer in a casserole dish. Core and slice apples. Layer on top of potatoes. Boil apple juice and then add in flour and water until thick. Drizzle sauce over apples. Garnish with cinnamon. Bake 45 mins at 350.

Serves 7.

# Pineapple Bars

## Crust:

*½ c. almonds, ground fine*
*¼ c. all-purpose gluten-free baking flour or brown rice flour*
*¼ c. water*
*1 c. granola crumbs*

Mix together with a fork in bottom of 9 x 13-inch pan. Press against bottom. Bake 5-10 minutes at 350 degrees.

## Filling:

*1-1/3 c. apple juice*
*1 c. dates*
*2½ c. crushed pineapple*
*2 tbsp unsweetened almond flour*
*1 tsp vanilla*
*Coconut for topping*

Blend water and dates in blender until smooth. Mix with other ingredients; pour over crust and sprinkle with coconut, then bake at 350 degrees for 15 minutes or until coconut is light brown. Cool well before cutting into desired squares.

Serves 4

# Sweet Quinoa Pudding

*2 c. cooked quinoa*
*1 c. apple juice*
*½ c. raisins*
*1 c. chopped water chestnuts*
*1½ tsp vanilla extract*
*Grated zest of 1 lemon*
*Pinch of ground cinnamon*
*1 kiwi fruit for garnish*

In a medium saucepan, combine quinoa, apple juice, raisins, water chestnuts, vanilla, lemon zest, and cinnamon. Cover pan and bring to a boil, then reduce heat and simmer for 15 minutes. Slice kiwi fruit. Divide pudding among 5 dessert dishes and top with kiwi fruit slices. Makes 5 servings.

To prepare quinoa:
thoroughly rinse ½ cup quinoa and drain. Combine quinoa with ½ cup water in a saucepan and bring to a boil. Cover pan, reduce heat to medium-low, and simmer for 10-15 minutes or until water is completely absorbed and grain is translucent.

Serves 3

# Brown Rice Pudding

*1 c. cooked brown rice*
*½ c. egg whites or substitute*
*2 c. rice or nut milk*
*½ tsp vanilla extract*
*½ c. raisins*
*½ tsp cinnamon*

In blender, mix milk, vanilla, eggs, and cinnamon. Spray 8 x 10-inch glass baking dish with non-stick spray. In a separate bowl, mix together brown rice raisins, and the blender mixture. Pour entire recipe into the baking dish; sprinkle with additional cinnamon and bake at 350 degrees for 35-40 minutes. Serve warm or cold.

Serves 4

# Raw Bread Pudding

*1-1/3 c. gluten-free bread crumbs*
*¼ c. ground flaxseed*
*¼ c. chopped almonds and sunflower seeds*
*1 c. chopped dates*
*2/3 c. orange juice*

Combine all ingredients. Mix well. Line a pie pan with wax paper and press mixture into pan. Cover and chill 5 hours. Remove pudding from pan and slice into thin wedges. Serve.

Serves 4

# Yam Soufflé

*2 c. cooked, mashed yams*
*1 c egg whites or egg substitute*
*1 tbsp cinnamon*
*1 tbsp grated orange peel*

Beat the egg whites to soft peak stage. Fold egg whites, cinnamon and orange peel into the yams. Divide into 4 individual soufflé dishes and bake at 350 degrees for 25 minutes. Serve immediately.

Serves 4.

# Orange Tart Pillows

*5 peeled, baked potatoes (about 2½ c.)*
*12 oz frozen orange juice*
*3 bananas*
*1 tsp vanilla*
*1/2 cup egg whites or egg substitute*

Preheat oven to 375 degrees. Bake potatoes for 35-40 mins. Beat the above list of ingredients together with the baked potatoes until smooth. Whisk in the "egg" and bake for another 15 minutes.

# Tahini Custard

*3 apples*
*½ c. raisins*
*2 c. apple juice*
*2-3 tbsp Erewhon sesame tahini*
*Pinch of salt*
*5 tbsp Erewhon agar flakes*
*2 c. water*

Wash, core and slice apples. Place in pot with liquids, tahini, sea salt, and agar. Mix well. Bring to a boil reduce heat to low and simmer 2-3 minutes. Chill in a shallow bowl until almost hardened. Place cooled mixture in blender; blend until smooth and creamy. Place custard back in serving bowl and chill once more before serving.

# Lemon Custard

*2 c. pear or apple juice*
*2 c. natural lemonade*
*2 bars agar-agar (or 3 tsp agar flakes)*
*Pinch of sea salt*
*1 tsp vanilla*
*1 c. lemon non-dairy frozen dessert*
*2 c. berries (raspberries, strawberries, or blueberries) (optional)*

Combine juice and lemonade in saucepan. Rinse agar bars; tear into 1-inch pieces and add to saucepan (or measure flakes and sprinkle on juice). Stir until agar softens. Bring mixture to light boil; lower heat and simmer for 10 minutes until agar dissolves. Add salt and vanilla. Add frozen dessert; stir to dissolve and pour into shallow, heat-proof dish. Place dish in refrigerator for 30 minutes until custard is set. Serve as is, or with berries. Serves 6.

# Applesauce Soufflé

*1¼ c. unsweetened applesauce*
*½ tsp cinnamon*
*2 tsp raisins*
*2/3 c. egg whites or substitute*

Preheat oven to 350 degrees. Blend applesauce and cinnamon. Spoon 1 tablespoon of applesauce into bottom of each of 4 (6-ounce) cups. Top with raisins. Beat eggs until stiff but not dry. Fold half into remaining applesauce and blend well. Fold remaining eggs into applesauce very gently. Spoon into cups and sprinkle tops with cinnamon. Bake about 15-20 minutes until puffed and brown. Serve immediately.  Serves 4.

# Banana Ambrosia

*1 lg ripe yellow banana*
*¼ c. pineapple or orange juice*
*1 lg ripe papaya*
*¼ c. vanilla or banana coconut milk ice cream*
*½ tsp vanilla extract*
*½ tsp coconut extract*
*Pinch of powdered ginger*
*1 tbsp sesame seeds or sesame tahini*

Peel and mash banana with fork. Place in bowl and add juice. Cut papaya in half; scoop out and discard seeds. Scoop papaya meat with spoon and add with ice cream to bowl. Mix in seasonings. Stir until well mixed.

# Fruit Kabobs

*2 Spanish blood oranges, small*
*navel oranges, or mandarins*
*12 kumquats or seedless grapes*
*2 thick slices fresh pineapple*
*1 lg ripe kiwi fruit*
*12 strawberries or pitted cherries*
*Watermelon, honeydew, or cantaloupe*
*(cut into 12 cubes)*

Cut fruit into bite-size slices, cubes or wedges. Spear fruit on thin skewers. Stand spears in bowl or bucket of crushed ice or use a hollowed out pineapple or watermelon filled with ice, to support the skewers.

Serves 12.

# Lychees Stuffed

*1¼ c. currants*
*¼ c. toasted sesame seeds*
*1 c. finely chopped dried apricots*
*1 tbsp sweet sherry*
*20 fresh or canned lychees (remove*
  *lychee stones from fresh ones, rinse*
  *canned lychees to remove excess sugar)*

Blend together currants, sesame seeds, dried apricots, and sherry. Stuff mixture into lychees.

Chill and serve.

# Banana Pie Cups

*Your favorite healthy cookies*
*So Delicious coconut vanilla pudding*
*Ripe bananas; sliced*
*Walnuts*
*Non-dairy whipped topping* (use Cashew
Cream recipe in this book)
*Cinnamon*

Crush cookies in a plastic bag and spoon
about 1/3 cup into the bottom of a glass.
Pour vanilla pudding over the top. Top
pudding with sliced bananas, then refrigerate if not serving immediately. Once
ready to serve, top bananas with walnuts,
whipped topping and cinnamon.

## Chestnut, Chocolate and Pear Dessert Pizza

*Gluten-Free Flatbread*
*Chestnut butter*
*1 bar of dark vegan chocolate or carob*
*2 small pears, chopped*

Preheat oven to 350. Place the flatbread on a baking sheet.   Spread the chestnut butter on the flatbread like a sauce. Grate the dark chocolate on top like cheese. Chop the pears and place them on the flatbread. Bake for 15 mins. Enjoy warm.

Serves 6.

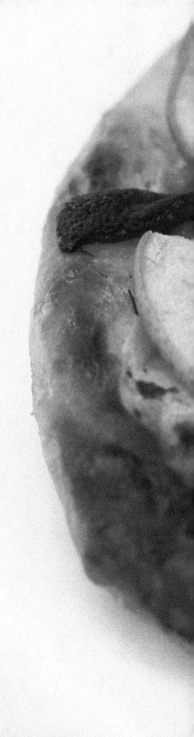

# Raw Vegan Ice Cream Bars

### *Ice Cream:*
*6 young coconuts*
*½ c. coconut water*
*1 tsp vanilla powder*
*½ c. coconut nectar*

Open the coconuts. Scrape out the meat. Combine the coconut meat, coconut water, vanilla and nectar in a blender until smooth. Transfer to an ice cream bar mold. Freeze overnight.

### *Cacao Shell:*
*2/3 cup raw cacao paste*
*½ c. liquid stevia*
*½ c. coconut butter*

Place all ingredients in a double boiler until melted.

Take the ice cream sticks out of the freezer. Dip in the chocolate. Hold the stick out for a few seconds until hardened. Place on baking paper to set. Repeat with all the ice cream bars. Once all bars have been dipped once, dip them for a second time to create a thicker shell. Put in freezer bags and store until ready to serve.

Serves 10.

# Banana Pineapple Ice Cream

*4 lg bananas cut into chunks*
*1 tsp vanilla*
*4 oz crushed pineapple, frozen and unsweetened*
  *(or any fruit you desire)*

Cut bananas into slices. Lay banana slices on cookie sheet and freeze. Pour pineapple into a bowl and freeze. Place the frozen fruit and vanilla in blender. Blend, stopping the motor to stir frequently until the mixture is smooth. Serve at once.

Serves 2.

# Chocolate Banana Ice Cream

*1 c. apple juice (for saucepan)*
*1 c. apple juice*
*3 tbsp all-purpose gluten-free baking flour or brown rice flour*
*½ c. carob powder*
*2 tbsp tahini*
*2 tbsp honey*
*4 ripe bananas*

Combine 1 cup apple juice in a saucepan. Blend in all-purpose gluten-free baking powder or brown rice flour and carob powder. Bring to a boil, stirring constantly. Pour into blender or food processor and blend with remaining ingredients. Chill well and freeze. Remove from freezer and blend in food processor until smooth.

Serves 8.

# Strawberry Ice Cream

*1 frozen banana, sliced*
*1 bunch of strawberries, frozen*
*2 tbsp coconut milk*
*1 tsp vanilla extract*

Blend all of the ingredients together in a blender until smooth. Scoop & Enjoy.

Serves 3.

# Apricot Sorbet

*2 ½ or 1 lb apricots*
*2 tsp chopped candied ginger*
*½ c. apple juice*
*1 c. water*
*2 tbsp orange juice*
*2 tbsp lemon juice*

Bring a large pot of water to a boil. Dip the apricots in the water for 1 min. Peel apricots. Then puree them in a blender with lemon juice, orange juice and ginger. Meanwhile, cook water and apple juice together on low heat. Bring to a boil for 5 minutes. Combine mixture. Freeze. Blend. Serve.

Serves 8.

## Pineapple Banana Sherbet

*½ c. orange juice*
*1 pineapple, chopped*
*1 banana*
*2 tbsp coconut nectar*
*4 tbsp fresh mint*
*1 tbsp fresh lime juice*

In a blender, mix together 2 tbsp of mint and orange juice until smooth. Blend in the rest of the ingredients (expect the additional 2 tbsp of mint for garnish) until smooth. Freeze overnight. Soften in refrigerator 1 hour before serving. Garnish with fresh mint.

Serves 4.

## Almond Tofu Pina Colada

*1 c. almond tofu, whipped in blender*
*1 c. diced fresh pineapple*
*1 c. grated fresh coconut*
*4 tbsp frozen apple juice*
*1 tsp vanilla*

Combine all ingredients. Chill. Spool into dessert dishes and garnish with kiwi fruit slices and fresh strawberries.

Serves 4.

# Frozen Cherry Mousse

*1 container almond or rice milk*
*½ c. frozen cherries*
*½ pkg agar-agar (gelatin substitute)*
*1 tbsp apple juice*
*1 egg white or egg substitute*
*½ tsp almond extract*

Pour rice milk in bowl; place in freezer. In food processor or blender, whip eggs with sweetener. Add frozen rice milk, cherries, agar-agar, almond extract. Whip 1 minute. Transfer to serving dish. Freeze 1-hour before serving.

# Pumpkin Ice Cream

*1 pkg agar-agar*
*¼ c. hot water*
*1 c. frozen orange juice*
*1 lb can organic pumpkin mix*
*½ tsp nutmeg*
*½ tsp ginger*
*½ tsp cinnamon*
*½ c. almond milk*

Dissolve agar-agar in hot water. Place orange juice, pumpkin, and spices in blender, then add rice milk. Put in shallow freezer trays and freeze. Stir often to break up ice crystals.
Serves 4-6.

# Pineapple Sorbet

*1 pineapple (sweet and ripe)*
*1 pt fresh strawberries, sliced*
*Fresh mint sprigs*

Blend pineapple until smooth in blender. Pour into a freezer container and freeze semi-hard. Then stir well and fold in sliced strawberries. Freeze overnight. When serving, garnish with fresh mint.

Serves 4.

# Banana Mousse

*6 ripe bananas*
*1½ c. unsweetened applesauce*
*2 tbsp carob powder*
*¼ tsp vanilla extract*

Blend all of the ingredients together in a blender until smooth. Refrigerate for 1 hour prior to serving.

Serves 4.

## Coconut Peach Freeze

*4 lg ripe peaches, peeled and finely diced*
*½ c.  canned coconut milk*
*½ c.  unsweetened peach or white grape juice*
*½ c.  unsweetened dried coconut flakes*

Freeze peached in a freezer bag overnight. Blend all ingredients together in a blender until smooth.

Serves 4.

## Tropical Fruit Tart

*3 c. coconut crust*
*2 mangoes, chopped*
*½ c. dried mangoes, chopped,*
*soaked 10 minutes and drained*
*2 c. fresh raspberries*
*1 c. fresh blueberries*
*1 c. fresh blackberries*

Distribute the coconut crust along the bottom and sides of a pie pan. Press down firmly to set. Freeze for 15 mins. Add the fresh and dried mangoes to a blender and mix until smooth. Spread the mango mixture on the bottom of the pie pan. Mix the berries in a bowl gently. Layer on top of the tart. Chill 2 hours before serving.

## Coconut Crust

*1½ c. unsweetened shredded dried coconut*
*1½ c. raw macadamia nuts or walnuts*
*½ tsp sea salt*
*½ c. pitted dates*

Place all ingredients in a blender and blender until the mixture because crumbs.

# Baked Apple

½ c. cranberry juice
1 baking apple
½ c. red wine
1 tsp apple juice
Pinch of cinnamon
1 tbsp of raisins

Core apple and stand it bottom down in baking dish. Sprinkle with sweetener and cinnamon, making sure some gets inside apple. Stuff raisins into the center of the apple. Pour juice and wine into baking dish around apple. Bake, uncovered, at 350 degrees for 20-25 minutes or until skin splits and the apple is tender.

# Strawberry Shortcake Muffins

2½ c. gluten free oats
1 c. coconut milk yogurt
½ c. egg whites or substitute
¾ c. xylitol sweetener
1½ tsp Rumford baking powder
½ tsp baking soda
1½ c. strawberries, diced,
½ c. strawberries, diced as garnish
1 tsp lemon juice

Set oven to 400. Mix all of the ingredients together in a blender until smooth. Pour into a bowl and mix in 1 ½ cup strawberries. Spoon the mixture into a 12 muffin tins. Place the remaining strawberries on top as garnish. Bake 25 mins.

# Raw Vegan Cheesecake with Blackberry Sauce

## Crust:
*2 cups almonds*
*1 cup dried dates*

Mix all ingredients together in a blender until smooth.

## Filling:
*3½ c. raw cashews, soaked*
*¾ c. lemon juice*
*¾ c. honey*
*1 c. coconut milk*
*½ c. water*
*1 vanilla bean*
*½ tsp sea salt*

Mix all ingredients together in a blender until smooth.

## Blackberry Sauce Topping
*Bunch of fresh blackberries*
*4 large dried  dates*
*2 tbsp coconut nectar*

Mix all ingredients together in a blender until smooth.

## Preperation:
Arrange crust in a pie pan. Layer filling on top. Finish off with the blackberry sauce. Cover and freeze overnight. Refrigerate for 1 hour prior to serving.

# Kiwi Coconut Dream

## *Coconut Cream Topping:*

*1 can coconut milk*
*1 tbsp coconut nectar*
*½ tsp vanilla*

Use 2 tbsp of coconut milk and set the rest aside for the kiwi blend. Whip all ingredients together with a hand mixer. Freeze while preparing the blend.

## *Kiwi Blend:*

*4 kiwi fruit*
*Remaining coconut milk*
*1 frozen banana, sliced*
*1 handful of spinach*
*½ cup vanilla yogurt*
*1 tsp honey*

Mix all ingredients together in blender and blend until smooth. Pour into small glasses and garnish with coconut cream.

# Chocolate Dipped Strawberries

*12 Strawberries*
*4 c. mon-dairy dark chocolate*

Melt the chocolate. Fill an ice tray with melted chocolate, put berries in and freeze them.

# Pina Colada Pops

*6 popsicle sticks*
*1 can pineapple chunks, in juice*
*1 banana*
*1 can coconut milk*
*½ tsp vanilla extract*

Blend and freeze. Serves 6.

# Vegan Mint Cookies & Cream Cheesecake

## *Crust:*
*1 cup crushed vegan chocolate cookies*
*1/2 cup crushed walnuts or almonds*
Mix ingredients together in a blender. Press crust into a pie dish.

## *Filling:*
*16 oz almond tofu*
*½ c. coconut milk*
*1 container vegan cream cheese*
*½ c. coconut nectar*
*5 vegan chocolate sandwich cookies*
*½ tsp peppermint extract*
*½ tsp sea salt*
*2 tbsp coconut milk*
*Garnish: 5 vegan chocolate sandwich cookies, crumbled*

Add all ingredients (except the garnish) to a blender until smooth. Pour filling over crust. Garnish with cookie crumbles. Cover and chill overnight. Serve with fresh mint and coconut whipped cream.

# Grilled Banana Boats

*1 ripe banana per person*
*Carob*
*Butterscotch*
*vegan peanut butter chips*
*mini vegan marshmallows*
*shredded coconut*
*or whatever toppings you prefer foil*

Slit the bananas lengthwise. Stuff them with any combination of toppings you desire. Wrap the bananas in foil.  Grill until toppings melt. Serve.

# Monkeys in a Blanket

*1 slice gluten-free, rice or potato bread*
*½ banana*
*½ tbsp almond milk*
*Cinnamon*
*Honey*

Preheat oven to 400 degrees. Roll bread flat with a rolling pin and trim crust. Spread with a thin layer of honey. Place banana on half of bread and wrap jelly roll fashion. Allow 1 tablespoon for each whole banana. Roll bread-covered banana in almond butter, sprinkle with cinnamon and bake for 15 minutes until crust is crisp and banana is hot and creamy.

# Whipped Tofu Cream

*8 oz almond tofu*
*¼ c. liquid Stevia*
*2 tsp vanilla extract*
*1 tsp lemon rind*
*1 tsp lemon juice*

Place all ingredients in blender and whip for 5 minutes. Stir 4 or 5 times then whip again for 5 minutes until creamy. Serves 4-6.

# Vanilla Fruit Cream

*1 c. millet*
*2 c. water*

Bring water to a boil; add millet and cook for 30-40 minutes.

*1 c. raw cashew pieces, washed*
*1 c. water*
*1 tsp salt*
*¼ c. coconut nectar*
*4 tbsp vanilla*

Blend cashews in water until smooth. Blend in other ingredients and add millet until smooth. Refrigerate unused portions. Goes great on fruit or bread.

# Revitalizing Chocolate Superfood Ganache

*4 c. chocolate sauce mix (see below for recipe)*
*3 tbsp Stem Cell Strong maca powder*
*1 tbsp spirulina*
*1 tsp cinnamon*
*½ c. hemp seeds*

Blend sauce, Stem Cell Strong maca powder, and spirulina well in high-powered blender until rich and creamy. Pour into 8-inch-square dish/non-stick pan and top with cinnamon and hemp seeds. Freeze for 1-hour; cut into desired shape. This makes a great snack for kids and can be cut into fun shapes. Makes 16 pieces.

## *Chocolate Sauce:*

*3 c. raw cacao nibs or 2 c. raw cacao powder*
*1 tbsp Stem Cell Strong maca powder*
*1 tbsp vanilla extract or 5 vanilla beans*
*¼ c. coconut milk*
*1 tsp cinnamon*
*2 c. coconut nectar*
*1 tsp sea salt*

Place all ingredients in a blender and blend until rich and creamy. Transfer to a squeeze bottle for easy garnishing or seal in a glass jar and store. VARIATION: add 1-cup almond milk for a creamy texture. Makes 2½ cups.

# INDEX...

# Beverages.

# Salads.

# Breakfast.

# Main Dishes.

# Desserts.

# About the Author

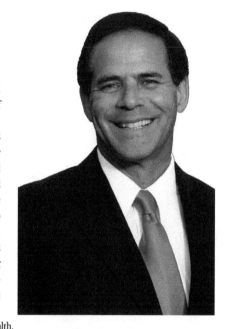

At the age of 23, Nick Delgado suffered a frightening transient ischemic attack (a mini stroke) that changed the course of his life forever. Subsequently, Nick devoted himself to becoming healthier, a fitness role model that would lead others to great health.

As a student, Nick was assigned to follow doctors in their hospital rounds. He was stunned by the large number of patients suffering from crippling joint diseases or affected by obesity and dying from strokes, degenerative heart diseases, diabetes and cancer. Since he also struggled with obesity and high blood pressure, he decided to put his own theorems to practice on his first patient... himself! After just 5 months, he reduced his body fat by 55 pounds and lowered his blood pressure from 200/90 to 110/70. This allowed him the freedom to discontinue his blood pressure medications. Nick Delgado graduated from the University of Southern California, with studies at Rancho Los Amigo Hospital, USC, Loma Linda University, California State Long Beach and Los Angeles as well as continued research with interventional endocrinology, hematology and physiology. He served as Director of the Pritikin Better Health Program of the Nathan Pritikin Longevity Center. Ongoing studies of participants in the Pritikin Plan were being monitored by Dr Massey of the Loma Linda School of Public Health.

Nick teamed with health experts and searched for consistent correlations with aging and symptomatic indications. He discovered new answers to age-old problems. During this period, he collaborated with many acclaimed physicians, including Denis Burkitt, M.D., Ernest Wynder, M.D., Arnold Fox, M.D., Thierry Hertoghe MD, Ron Klatz MD, and Ron Rothenberg MD.

Nick Delgado wrote his thesis on a comprehensive study of 693 people, which he conducted as part of a wellness program provided through seminars of world-renown motivational speaker, Anthony Robbins with Mastery University. Nick has been presenting the concepts of the Delgado Protocol to audiences worldwide. During the past 30 years he has educated over 100,000 people on topics such as eyes open relaxation of the unconscious mind, aging, wellness, sexual health, using cellular hematology, oxidative stress analysis, carotid artery scans, blood lipids testing and biochemical hormones. Dr. Nick has been a keynote speaker in Japan, Malaysia, Toronto, Canada and was awarded "Best Speaker" at the International Anti-Aging Congress in South Africa.

Nick Delgado is a major contributing author to Anti-Aging Clinical Protocols published by A4M. He is a contributor to scientifically reviewed books, with research on hormones, herbs, and lifestyle therapies. He is also the holder of the World Strength Endurance record lifting 50,640 lbs in one hour. Dr Delgado is currently training to break the World Record for aging (114 for men), now 57 years young. Nick Delgado is an inspiration to those athletes who think their career ends at age 40. As one of the world's primary experts on anti-aging, Dr. Nick has lectured physicians and healthcare professionals at conferences at over 50 major conventions with nonprofit education serving over 22,000 doctors.

CPSIA information can be obtained
at www.ICGtesting.com
Printed in the USA
BVHW010005300919
559488BV00002BA/7/P